Crime Victim's Guide to Justice

Crime Victim's Guide to Justice

Third Edition

MARY L. BOLAND
Attorney at Law

SPHINX® PUBLISHING
AN IMPRINT OF SOURCEBOOKS, INC.®
NAPERVILLE, ILLINOIS
www.SphinxLegal.com

Third Edition: 2008

Published by: **Sphinx® Publishing, An Imprint of Sourcebooks, Inc.®**
Naperville Office
P.O. Box 4410
Naperville, Illinois 60567-4410
(630) 961-3900
Fax: 630-961-2168
www.sourcebooks.com
www.SphinxLegal.com

This publication is designed to provide accurate and authoritative information in regard to the subject matter covered. It is sold with the understanding that the publisher is not engaged in rendering legal, accounting, or other professional service. If legal advice or other expert assistance is required, the services of a competent professional person should be sought.

From a Declaration of Principles Jointly Adopted by a Committee of the American Bar Association and a Committee of Publishers and Associations

This product is not a substitute for legal advice.

Disclaimer required by Texas statutes.

Library of Congress Cataloging-in-Publication Data

Boland, Mary L.
  Crime victim's guide to justice / by Mary L. Boland. -- 3rd ed.
    p. cm.
  Includes index.
  ISBN 978-1-57248-655-3 (pbk. : alk. paper) 1. Victims of crimes--Legal status, laws, etc.-- United States--Popular works. 2. Criminal procedure--United States--Popular works. I. Title.
  KF9763.B65 2008
  344.7303'288--dc22
                          2008012742

Printed and bound in the United State of America.
SB 10 9 8 7 6 5 4 3 2 1

ACKNOWLEDGMENTS

Many people contributed over several years to the information that eventually made its way into this book. I most want to thank Katherine A. Newell, an excellent paralegal and researcher, for her time and invaluable assistance in gathering, typing, and editing the compilation of statutory materials cited in the first edition of this book.

CONTENTS

USING SELF-HELP LAW BOOKS

Before using a self-help law book, you should realize the advantages and disadvantages of doing your own legal work and understand the challenges and diligence that this requires.

The Growing Trend

Rest assured that you will not be the first or only person handling your own legal matter. For example, in some states, more than 75% of divorces and other cases have at least one party representing him- or herself. Because of the high cost of legal services, this is a major trend and many courts are struggling to make it easier for people to represent themselves. However, some courts are not happy with people who do not use attorneys and refuse to help them in any way. For some, the attitude is, "Go to the law library and figure it out for yourself."

We write and publish self-help law books to give people an alternative to the often complicated and confusing legal books found in most law libraries. We have made the explanations of the law as simple and easy to understand as possible. Of course, unlike an attorney advising an individual client, we cannot cover every conceivable possibility.

Whenever you shop for a product or service, you are faced with various levels of quality and price. In deciding what product or service to buy, you make a cost/value analysis on the basis of your willingness to pay and the quality you desire.

Cost/Value Analysis

When buying a car, you decide whether you want transportation, comfort, status, or sex appeal. Accordingly, you decide among such choices as a Focus, Lincoln, Rolls Royce, or Porsche. Before making a decision, you usually weigh the merits of each option against the cost.

When you get a headache, you can take a pain reliever (such as aspirin) or visit a medical specialist for a neurological examination. Given this choice, most people, of course, take a pain reliever, since it costs only pennies, whereas a medical examination costs hundreds of dollars and takes a lot of time. This is usually a logical choice because it is rare to need anything more than a pain reliever for a headache. But in some cases, a headache may indicate a brain tumor and failing to see a specialist right away can result in complications. Should everyone with a headache go to a specialist? Of course not, but people treating their own illnesses must realize that they are betting on the basis of their cost/value analysis of the situation. They are taking the most logical option.

The same cost/value analysis must be made when deciding to do one's own legal work. Many legal situations are very straightforward, requiring a simple form and no complicated analysis. Anyone with a little intelligence and a book of instructions can handle the matter without outside help.

But there is always the chance that complications are involved that only an attorney would notice. To simplify the law into a book like this, several legal cases often must be condensed into a single sentence or paragraph. Otherwise, the book would be several hundred pages long and too complicated for most people. However, this simplification necessarily leaves out many details and nuances that would apply to special or unusual situations. Also, there are many ways to interpret most legal questions. Your case may come before a judge who disagrees with the analysis of our authors.

Therefore, in deciding to use a self-help law book and to do your own legal work, you must realize that you are making a cost/value analysis. You have decided that the money you will save in doing it yourself outweighs the chance that your case will not turn out to your satisfaction. Most people handling their own simple legal matters never have a problem, but occasionally people find that it ended up costing them more to have an attorney straighten out the situation than it would have if they had hired an attorney in the beginning. Keep this in mind if you decide to handle your own case, and be sure to consult an attorney if you feel you might need further guidance.

Local Rules

The next thing to remember is that a book that covers the law for the entire nation, or even for an entire state, cannot possibly include every procedural difference of every county court. Whenever possible, we provide the exact form needed; however, in some areas, each county, or even each judge, may require unique forms and procedures. In our state books, our forms usually cover the majority of counties in the state, or provide examples of the type of form that will be required. In our national books, our forms are sometimes even more general in nature, but are designed to give a good idea of the type of form that will be needed in most locations. Nonetheless, keep in mind that your state, county, or judge may have a requirement, or use a form, that is not included in this book.

You should not necessarily expect to be able to get all the information and resources you need solely from within the pages of this book. This book will serve as your guide, giving you specific information whenever possible and helping you to find out what else you will need to know. This is just like if you decided to build your own backyard deck. You might purchase a book on how to build decks. However, such a book would not include the building codes and permit requirements of every city, town, county, and township in the nation; nor would it include the lumber, nails, saws, hammers, and other materials and tools you would need to actually build the deck. You would use the book as your guide, and then do some work and research involving such matters as whether you need a permit of some kind, what type and grade of wood are available in your area, whether to use hand tools or power tools, and how to use those tools.

Changes in the Law

Besides being subject to local rules and practices, the law is subject to change at any time. The courts and the legislatures of all fifty states are constantly revising the laws. It is possible that while you are reading this book, some aspect of the law is being changed.

In most cases, the change will be of minimal significance. A form will be redesigned, additional information will be required, or a waiting period will be extended. As a result, you might need to revise a form, file an extra form, or wait out a longer time period; these types of changes will not usually affect the outcome of your case. On the other hand, sometimes a major part of the law is changed, the entire law in a particular area is rewritten, or a case that was the basis of a central legal point is overruled. In such instances, your entire ability to pursue your case may be impaired.

To help you with local requirements and changes in the law, be sure to review Appendix C on "Legal Research."

Again, you should weigh the value of your case against the cost of an attorney and make a decision as to what you believe is in your best interest.

INTRODUCTION

Nearly everyone will be affected by crime in some way during their lifetime. Television brings trials into our homes, and court-watching has become commonplace. Yet, beyond the media hype, a victim's rights are a mystery to most, and no one can exercise rights they do not know exist. Victims, their families, and supporters must learn about these laws and learn how and when to apply this knowledge.

This book will help you understand the criminal and civil court systems from the victim's perspective. It is intended to teach you how the criminal justice system functions, what your rights are as a victim, how to find help, and how to make the people who make the decisions about your case accountable to you. This book is also intended to help victims who are considering filing a civil lawsuit. It is a starting place, a basic guide to the maze of our court systems.

Do not hesitate to demand justice as you travel from victim to survivor. And when your journey is complete, gather strength from your experience and think about how you can have an impact on your community to improve the treatment of future victims.

Chapters 1 and 2 explain your general rights as a crime victim and how to get help. Chapters 3 through 9 will help you navigate the criminal justice process. Chapter 10 explains your privacy rights. Chapter 11 explains the options to recover your losses. Chapter 12 discusses the civil court process, and Chapter 13 provides some tips for working with lawyers. The glossary will help you understand the legal jargon used in all the chapters. Most italicized words throughout the text are in the glossary.

Appendix A lists street and Internet addresses and telephone numbers that may be useful to you. Appendix B discusses the basic rights of victims and provides you with laws that may be important to your case. Appendix C provides some basic information about legal research, in the event you want to go beyond what is covered in this book. Appendix D is a case management guide to help you organize your papers for trial, and Appendix E includes examples of forms to assist you in navigating the legal process.

THE VICTIM IN THE CRIMINAL JUSTICE SYSTEM

1

The Rights of Victims

In colonial times, when a person committed a crime, it was considered to be an injury to the victim and the victim was entitled to prosecute the case. This system favored wealthy victims, however, because poorer victims did not have the financial resources to seek justice. To make the process fairer, the government took over the responsibility of prosecuting a person accused of committing a crime. Crimes began to be considered public wrongs committed against the community, rather than private wrongs committed only against the individual victim. However, victims began to be considered a piece of evidence in the process, and they lost the ability to have meaningful participation in the process of justice.

For example, even though the crime is committed against the victim, the victim is often seen by the criminal justice system as peripheral to the case. The victim is not a party to the case, and cannot force the prosecutor to act on his or her behalf. The law does not permit a victim to privately prosecute a criminal case. For many years, victims did not have any legal rights at all. They were expected to appear and give testimony, often without much preparation by the prosecutor. It may take months, even years, for a case to come to trial, and many victims just dropped out of the criminal court process.

In the 1970s, the crime victims' rights movement sought changes in the system to increase the rights of crime victims. President Reagan commissioned a task force on victims that produced a scathing report about the treatment of victims in the system and suggested numerous reforms. Improvements over the last twenty years include:

- rape evidence collection kits;

- better training of medical personnel;

- removal of victims' personal information from the public records;

- notification of victims when the perpetrator of a crime is released on bail;

- education of victims in court procedures;

- safe waiting areas for victims;

- limiting continuances;

- victims not being required to testify as to their addresses; and,

- assigning a single prosecutor for the entirety of the criminal case.

Rape Evidence Collection Kits

Before the presidential task force changed medical protocols, rape was not considered an injury by many hospitals. Rape evidence collection kits and the training of hospital staff are modifications that have improved the experiences of the victim. The kits standardized the type and quantity of evidence collected, so that all medical procedures and evidentiary requirements could be completed in most cases at the initial emergency room visit.

Training of Medical Personnel

The training of medical personnel improved the understanding of the dynamics of certain kinds of crimes, which resulted in more sensitive treatment of victims. For example, prior to training, some medical personnel blamed domestic violence victims for the crimes, asking, "Why didn't you leave, if this has happened before?" or "What were you two fighting about this time?" This made victims more reluctant to report the true nature of the injury. Some preferred to say that they had "fallen down stairs," or "bumped into a door," rather than be humiliated with questions or comments from medical staff. Training on the dynamics of domestic violence, including the cycle of violence often present in these cases, has improved the treatment of victims and made them more likely to report these types of crimes.

Public Records

Prior to the changes in the law, the victim's name and address were available as public records. As a result, victims were easily harassed by the media, insurance and security salesmen, and the perpetrators of the crimes. Today, the release of the victim's address on public records may be prohibited. Some states also provide victims with protection from the assailant's intimidation by adding new crimes for communication or harassment of a witness, and increasing penalties for offenders who harass witnesses prior to trial. In some states, the offender's bail may be revoked if he or she violates the condition prohibiting him or her from contacting the victim pending trial, and he or she could return to jail until trial.

Bail Conditions

After being arrested, some offenders continue to harass their victims, either from a jail phone or after being released on bail (often without the victim being made aware of the release). When releasing the accused on bail, judges were not always aware of continued threats or harassment of the victim. Today, prosecutors more often confer with victims regarding danger issues and bail conditions. In some states, information about bail release is available, and intimidation of the victim may specifically be cause for the revocation of bail.

Preliminary Hearing

Prior to changes in the law, victims did not know what was involved in a preliminary hearing, how long it would take, or how they should prepare. Now, victims are entitled to know about the procedures. Prosecutors and victim-witness personnel take the time to prepare the victim before the different parts of the trial.

Safe Waiting Areas

Victims and assailants often came in contact with each other in the hallways surrounding the preliminary hearings, causing the victim continued distress. Victims are now entitled to wait in areas that minimize contact with the defendant.

Continuances

Repeated continuances can cost the victim unnecessary expenses such as hiring a babysitter, leaving work, and parking. Some states require judges to consider the impact of continuances on a victim.

Testimony

Prior to 1982, refusing to disclose your home and work address could result in being held in contempt of court. In order to maintain the privacy of the victim, some states prohibit compelling a victim to testify as to his or her address and other identifying information unless there is a valid legal reason.

Testifying can be a frightening experience, especially for a child. Today, victims may be entitled to have a support person present in court; child victims may be entitled to specialized consideration.

Prosecutors

Prosecutors could be repeatedly reassigned before the trial even began. Victims would have to tell each new prosecutor the same detailed story and would not receive notification of continuances. As a result of new laws, some prosecutor's offices have a single prosecutor stay with the case from start to finish in certain kinds of cases. Victims are also entitled to receive information on continuances.

These are just some of the improvements that have evolved since the 1982 task force report.

Constitutional Rights

The most important right that one can hold under the criminal justice system is a *constitutional right*. Defendants have had constitutional rights since the founding of our country, but even though the former president's task force recommended the addition of a Crime Victim's Amendment as long ago as 1982, victims' rights are still not constitutionally protected. Instead, many states have passed state constitutional amendments that grant victims the right to be treated with fairness and dignity in their state's criminal justice system, while the remainder of the states provide statutory rights to victims. In fact, over the last twenty-five years, the victim's rights movement has resulted in more than thirty thousand laws nationwide to improve the status of victims.

The Federal Law

In 2004, the federal government passed the *Crime Victims' Rights Act*, which established expansive rights for crime victims at the federal level. (See 18 U.S.C. §3771.) This act amends the federal law to grant crime victims specified rights, including the following.

1. The right to be reasonably protected from the accused.

2. The right to reasonable, accurate, and timely notice of any public court proceeding or any parole proceeding involving the crime or of any release or escape of the accused.

3. The right not to be excluded from any such public court proceeding, unless the court, after receiving clear and convincing evidence, determines that testimony by the victim would be materially altered if the victim heard other testimony at that proceeding.

4. The right to be reasonably heard at any public proceeding in the district court involving release, plea, sentencing, or any parole proceeding.

5. The reasonable right to confer with the attorney for the government in the case.

6. The right to full and timely restitution as provided in law.

7. The right to proceedings free from unreasonable delay.

8. The right to be treated with fairness and with respect for the victim's dignity and privacy.

The act also requires prosecutors to notify victims that they can seek the advice of an attorney with respect to the rights established by the act. One of the most significant changes in federal law produced by this act is its addition of enforcement provisions. For example, under the act, either the crime victim or the government may assert the victim's rights in the district court. If, after making a motion in the district court, a victim or the government is not satisfied that the victim's rights have been recognized, either may file a petition with the court of appeals. The court of appeals must issue a decision within seventy-two hours of filing, and if it denies the relief sought, must state clearly on the record in a written opinion the reasons for the denial.

The federal legal changes are having an immediate effect. In 2006, a federal appellate court held that victims have a right to speak at sentencing hearings and not just submit victim impact statements. Most importantly, the court decided that if the trial court failed to grant victims that right, the remedy was a new sentencing hearing at which the victims could speak. The case involved a father and son who defrauded numerous victims out of their money. At the father's sentencing, several victims spoke, but later at the son's sentencing the trial court decided that victims would not be permitted to speak. The United States Court of Appeals for the Ninth Circuit reversed the trial court's decision. (See *Kenna v. U.S. District Court for the Central District of California*, 435 F.3d 1011 (9th Cir. 2006).)

The Rights of Crime Victims

Each state has its own list of crime victim protections. As a group, the basic rights of victims are:

- the right to information;

- the right to notice and to participate;

- the right to be protected;

- the right to compensation and restitution;

- the right to privacy; and,

- the right to civil justice.

The Right to Information

A victim has the right to know what his or her rights are, what medical, social, and financial services or programs he or she may be entitled to, and what is happening in the criminal justice system. Many states provide brochures or information cards to victims at the first contact with the police or prosecutor's office that list these rights. The victim may be provided with a name, address, and contact phone number of the police officer or prosecutor assigned to the case. Larger police departments may have victim-assistance officers who keep the victim informed as to the status of the case and provide any notices or written follow-up to the victim on victim assistance programs, such as available crisis intervention or crime victims' compensation (sometimes called *reparation*) programs.

Although information may be automatically provided, some states may require the victim to request to be kept informed of case progress. Send letters to the police and prosecutor requesting to be kept informed. These letters also serve to keep officials informed of your address and other contact information. (For a sample letter to the police and prosecutor, see form 1, p.159, and form 2, p.160, in Appendix E.) Case information may include the status of the investigation, the arrest, the release of the accused on bail, the filing of charges (or decision not to file), the commencement of prosecution, hearings and continuances, the sentencing date, and the judge's decision or a judgment of conviction and release of the offender.

The Right to Notice and to Participate

The role of the victim in the criminal justice system is expanding, and victims are entitled to participate in criminal proceedings in every state. In order for a victim to exercise a right to be present or participate, he or she must know it exists. This right includes getting advance notice of hearings or proceedings at which the victim is entitled to be present.

In some states, the victim is permitted to present testimony at the bail hearing regarding his or her fear of harm or threats by the defendant. In other states, the prosecutor is required to confer or consult with the victim prior to making charges or plea decisions.

In many states, the victim is now entitled to be present at court proceedings on the same basis as the defendant. In some states, the victim's welfare is considered in determining whether continuances will be granted. Some states also permit the victim to bring a support person into court while he or she testifies.

All states permit some victim input into consideration of the sentence. Because the vast majority of criminal cases are resolved by plea bargain, the sentencing hearing may be the only opportunity for the victim to speak to the judge about the crime. In many states, the prosecutor is required to consult with the victim prior to plea negotiations or agreement (this does not mean that the victim can force the prosecutor to take any particular action; it only requires the prosecutor to consider the victim's position). Also, written *victim impact statements* are often included in the materials the judge considers prior to approving a plea or determining a sentence. In some states, the victim is entitled to present the statement in person and to recommend an appropriate sentence.

Victim impact information is also crucial in consideration of parole, pardon, or commutation of an offender's sentence, and many states permit the written and oral presentation of a victim impact statement to parole officials. Victims are entitled to know if the offender escapes and if he or she is recaptured. In order to exercise this right, victims must keep corrections officials informed of their address. See form 3 (p.161) in Appendix E for a sample letter to corrections officials.

The Right to Be Protected

A victim has the right to be protected throughout the criminal justice process. This may mean that he or she is entitled to a protective order that prohibits the accused from making any contact with the victim or victim's family; it includes consideration of victim safety in bail decisions. Victims should be given information on the right to be free from intimidation while cooperating with law enforcement in the prosecution of their case. Secure or safe waiting areas are to be provided to victims while attending court proceedings to minimize their contact with the defendant and the defendant's family and friends. The police or other criminal justice personnel may provide protective assistance, and intimidation of the victim can be a criminal act in all states. In some states, the prosecutor may specifically request revocation of the defendant's bond for intimidating, threatening, or harming the victim or the victim's family.

The Right to Compensation and Restitution

Part of holding an offender accountable is the duty to pay for the harm he or she has caused the victim. The victim in all states has the right to *crime victim compensation* through state-run programs that reimburse some of the out-of-pocket losses incurred as a result of the crime. Each state's requirements differ. For example, in one state, the victim must report the crime to police within seventy-two hours. In other states, the law only applies to violent crimes. The attorney general's office of each state will be able to provide you with the necessary information on how and where to file for crime victim's compensation. In addition, many states mandate, and all states require consideration of, restitution to the victim for his or her losses.

The Right to Privacy

One of the reasons given when victims fail to report their crimes to police is a fear of a loss of privacy. A basic right of victims is to keep their privacy intact. Many states provide special privacy laws in sexual assault and child abuse cases, and many also provide for special privacy rights for counseling.

The Right to Civil Justice

The goals of the criminal justice system are to make the public whole. This may mean holding an offender accountable by punishing him or her or requiring him or her to make restitution to the victim for certain losses. But it is the civil justice system that can provide a victim with a greater chance to recover for the losses suffered due to crime.

Every crime is a public wrong, but it is also a private wrong. Private, or *civil*, wrongs are called *torts*. The crime of battery, for example, is also a tort of battery. Torts are the basis for personal injury and property damage civil lawsuits. This means that every crime victim is entitled to file a civil lawsuit to seek money damages for the pain, suffering, and economic losses caused by the crime. Some states also permit victims to file civil restitution liens against the defendant, and to file claims for the offender's profits that he or she may make through selling the rights to his or her story, writing a book, or even selling paintings, as one serial killer did.

In addition to these basic rights, many states provide for other general rights. For example, court procedures can be lengthy. Property taken as evidence or recovered by police in the possession of the offender should be promptly returned to the victim once its evidentiary purpose has been met. In some states, this means that once the police photograph or the crime lab analyzes the materials, they should be returned to the victim. In a few states, officials are required to return property within five to ten days after requested by the victim, unless good cause can be shown why the property cannot be returned. Many states provide special rights for certain groups of victims, such as sexual assault or domestic violence victims.

Finding these laws, however, can be very time-consuming. For more on how to find the laws in your state, see Appendixes A and B. One particularly good resource for finding the law is the VictimLaw database maintained by the *National Center for Victims of Crime*. It can be accessed at **www.victimlaw.info/victimlaw**. The database includes search topics on the following rights of crime victims:

- the right to attend criminal justice proceedings;

- the right to apply for compensation;

- the right to be heard and participate in criminal justice proceedings;

- the right to be informed of proceedings and events in the criminal justice process, of legal rights and remedies, and of available services;

- the right to protection from intimidation and harassment;

- the right to restitution from the offender;

- the right to prompt return of personal property seized as evidence;

- the right to a speedy trial; and,

- the right to enforcement of these rights.

Family Members and Loved Ones

The attack on the victim will often have serious consequences for the victim's loved ones. Anger and disbelief are common feelings. When a victim is killed as a result of the crime, the family and loved ones often suffer severe emotional, and even physical, effects from the crime.

For many years, these family members and loved ones did not have a role in the criminal justice system. In most cases, they were not witnesses and so could not testify. They were not given notices of court hearings and often did not know exactly what was happening in the case. They were not asked how they felt to have a plea bargain struck, and they sometimes did not even know the sentence at all. (A *plea bargain* is where the defendant is allowed to plead guilty to some or all of the charges, often in return for the state's recommendation of a particular sentence, which is likely to be lower than if the defendant went to trial and lost.)

Today this has changed, and if a victim dies, the family or a designated person steps into the victim's shoes and has the same rights normally granted to the victim in that state or jurisdiction. Thus, if your family member or loved one was killed, you become the victim for purposes of notification and the right to participate in the criminal justice system.

Witnesses

Witnesses have many of the same concerns about privacy and safety that victims have. In an effort to encourage witnesses to come forward and testify, the law has included witnesses in some of the protections given to crime victims.

Technology and Crime

As technology improves, so does the government's efforts to deal with crime and criminals. This technology can be used to help prevent crime; it can also make it easier to learn about crime and criminals. For example, federal, state, and local governments have begun to use the World Wide Web to provide an enormous amount of crime information to anyone with access to the Internet. Technology can also assist victims in participating in their cases—for example, a telephone may enable you to register for automatic notice of your pending court case or to be notified automatically of an offender's escape or release from prison. Also, agencies that provide services to crime victims can now be found in great numbers on the Web. (See Appendix A for a list of websites).

With access to the Internet, *crime mapping* can tell you the crime story of a neighborhood at a glance. You may also be able to find out where registered sex offenders live or the status of an incarcerated convict. But not everything is positive about new technology. Cybercrimes and sexual exploitation of children are two of the negative sides of increased access to the Internet.

Cybercrime

One type of crime that has become the subject of national attention is the exploitation of children online. Another involves what has been called *identity theft*, in which the criminal steals the identity of the victim and begins using the victim's name, address, or credit information.

Child Exploitation Online

Exploiting children through the Internet has become a pastime of online sexual predators who use their computers and the Internet to obtain photographs of child pornography. These offenders also exchange names and addresses of other predators and of potential child victims. The Internet also allows these online predators to enter the home of a child who is using a computer. Children may believe they are chatting with someone their own age and may share private information about themselves and their families. The predators attempt to develop an online relationship with the child, then attempt to meet the child somewhere in person. Children may not wish to report the contacts to parents because they do not wish to lose their online privileges.

In 1998, the *National Center for Missing & Exploited Children* began a national clearinghouse for tips and leads regarding the sexual exploitation of children. More information on this issue can be obtained from the National Center at **www.missingkids.com**. Reports can be made online at **www.missingkids.com/ cybertip**, or on the twenty-four-hour National Child Pornography Tipline at 800-843-5678.

Identity Theft

Although fraudulent use of another's identity occurred before the Internet became popular, technology has made it much easier for this type of thief to steal. In 1998, the federal government made identity theft a federal crime, and the majority of states have also passed laws criminalizing identify theft. The *Federal Trade Commission* (FTC) operates the Identity Theft Hotline and Data Clearinghouse at **www.ftc.gov/idtheft.** You may also call the FTC at 877-438-4338 for more information about this crime, its prevention, and its remedies.

Technology and Victims

Technology can help victims participate in their cases.

EXAMPLE
In the Oklahoma bombing of April 1995 in which 168 victims died and over five hundred more were injured, new technology allowed victims in Oklahoma to watch the defendants' trials in Colorado on closed-circuit television.

Closed-circuit television has also been used to assist child victims in testifying to their abuse. Technology is also helping domestic violence victims. Cellular phones, house perimeter alarms, and electronic bracelets (which limit or track offenders' movements) can help protect victims of domestic violence or stalking.

Automating Notice and Information

The responsibility for notifying victims of their rights in the criminal justice process usually falls to victim/witness staff in prosecutor's offices and larger police departments. The first contact might be in person or a telephone call or a letter is mailed to the victim's address. Sometimes, victims have to specifically request information on their case. But today, technology has improved the victim's right to know.

The federal government has adopted an automated victim notification system for federal cases, and more than forty states provide for automated victim notification for state cases. According to the national victim notification service, over 1.3 million victims have been served on the federal level as of September 2007.

Most automated victim notification programs are similar. The technology works by accessing information from prosecutors, court clerks, and jails or prisons, and then downloading the information into databases. The program only requires that the victim have access to a telephone or the Internet to use it. For telephone use, the caller is asked for the offender's name or state criminal identification number. The program can provide the offender's custody status, including whether he or she has escaped, and court dates, times, locations, and continuances. In addition, victims can usually call the system on a toll-free number. Information is normally provided in a number of languages.

After obtaining the offender's court and custody status, the caller can register a telephone number that will be automatically called to provide notice of changes in status, such as when the offender is released or transferred back into the community. Some programs can also provide information through an automatic notification letter to a registered victim.

More information on automated victim notification can be found by visiting **www.vinelink.com** twenty-four hours a day or by calling VINE, the company that provides notification systems in the majority of states (and other countries), at 800-865-4314 and asking for the phone number for a participating VINE program in your area. Your jurisdiction may not use VINE as its vendor, so you may also do a search for "automated victim notification" in your jurisdiction on the Internet, or contact your local police, prosecutor, or state's attorney general's office for more information. The federal government has a victim notification system that provides federal crime victims with information on scheduled court events, as well as the outcome of those court events. It also provides victims with information on the offender's custody status and release. Further information can be found by calling 866-365-4968 or by accessing the Internet website at **www.notify.usdoj.gov**.

Enforcing Your Rights

What happens if your rights are not respected? The reality is that while victim's rights have come a long way, they are still not routinely enforceable to the extent they need to be. Still, improvements are being made each year to hold accountable those who are charged with the responsibility of providing victims with their rights to information, notice, and an opportunity to participate.

The Federal Department of Justice has established an ombudsman program to help victims in federal cases. The *Office of the Victim's Rights Ombudsman* responds to complaints by crime victims whose cases are in the federal court system. The goal is to correct the problem so that it does not reoccur and to take action, when necessary, to correct the employee so that the next victim does not experience the same problem. Forms and additional information can be found at **www.usdoj.gov/usao/eousa/vr/index.html**.

States use varying approaches to enforce the rights of crime victims. Some have an ombudsman like the federal government; others provide for a victim's office within the governor's office, attorney general's office, or other state agency. Most try to resolve the complaint by providing the information requested or a referral for services. Most also work with the complained-of agency to improve conditions for victims. Some have no enforcement power; others have a more formal, investigatory function.

GETTING HELP

2

The Impact of Crime

Not all crimes are alike, nor are all victims affected the same way by crime, but most victims do experience some sense of loss as a result of crime. Victims may have physical, emotional, and psychological injuries, as well as loss of property. Even if the crime perpetrated against you or your loved one is relatively minor from the standpoint of the legal system, it may have a profound impact on you.

Many victims report feeling powerless, fearful, guilty, confused, and angry. Realize that recovering from the crime may take some time. Short-term crisis intervention will help, but it may take a year or longer to regain a sense of normalcy in your life. You may feel overwhelmed by the crime against you and may not think you have enough energy to fight for your rights, but there are ways.

There are many avenues that you can look to for support. If you have a religious or spiritual advisor, check with him or her for resources. Sometimes a friend can offer rest, comfort, and assistance, but often friends and family members need help understanding the crime or the criminal justice system themselves, and they may not be able to give you the kind of help you need. The services of a psychiatrist, psychologist, psychotherapist, or counselor who is trained to help crime victims may better suit your needs. The title of the helper is not as important as whether that person is competent to deal with your specific kind of case.

Make sure you ask about credentials and experience in handling cases like yours. Talk with the person and then make your decision. Meeting with a trained person who can help you make sense of what you are feeling can also help you gather the strength you need to stay and fight for your rights.

In 1984, the federal government passed the *Victims of Crime Act*, which provides funding to states to develop and initiate programs for crime victims. Today, many states have funded programs that provide information, counseling, and advocacy to crime victims. These programs can provide you with crisis intervention through hotlines, explain financial procedures, help acquaint you with court procedures, and provide information on local shelters and centers.

Victim-Assistance Programs

Victim-assistance personnel act as a liaison between the victim and the criminal justice system, and their services are free of charge. Many larger police departments and prosecutor's offices employ victim-assistance, also called *victim-witness*, personnel. Because these programs are funded locally, they may be very thorough and comprehensive, or they may be limited to providing information only. Usually, at a minimum, these persons can help to explain local procedures and will often have local resource information for your referral.

Hotline Services

Some public or private agencies have established *hotlines* to assist crime victims. These phone lines may operate twenty-four hours a day and are usually called *crisis lines*. Often, a trained staff member or volunteer can help ease your immediate concerns over the phone and set up an appointment for you to see a counselor or refer you to another resource. These hotlines may also be set up for information and referral only. Many hotlines provide confidentiality, but before leaving any identifying information, make sure you understand what kind of confidentiality is offered by the hotline service.

Crisis Counseling

Many states provide funding for agencies to provide some counseling and peer support to victims of crime. Rape crisis centers and domestic violence shelters are a few examples. Many programs also serve the families and significant others of the victims.

Programs may offer a number of free counseling sessions for victims and significant others, or may charge according to a sliding fee scale based on your ability to pay. The programs may also run support groups for victims to join together and talk about their situations. If you do choose a program that has a charge, remember that you may be able to file an insurance claim or seek reimbursement through your state's crime victim compensation program, so keep a record of your billing.

Many crime victims are concerned about their privacy rights when they share intimate fears and details of the crime with a counselor or in a support group. In recognition of the victim's privacy concerns, some states provide legal protection for the victim's privacy rights, and counseling programs are often available on a confidential basis. Before you choose, make sure you understand what kind of confidentiality is available through that person or agency.

The Crime Victim Advocate

A *crime victim's advocate* is a person who can provide information, assistance, and referral services. Some can provide services immediately after the crime, such as rape victim advocates who go to the hospital with the victim. Advocates can be volunteers or staff members of large or small private or public agencies. Most have attended some kind of training on court systems and processes and should be able to provide you with information on the procedures that will apply to your case.

Lawyers for Crime Victims

The concept of lawyers for victims in criminal court is relatively new, with the first legal clinics established throughout the country in 2003. Currently there are eight legal clinics that are a part of the *National Crime Victim Law Institute* (NCVLI) (**www.lclark.edu/org/ncvli**).

For civil lawsuits, the *National Crime Victim Bar Association* provides crime victims with referrals to lawyers specializing in victim-related lawsuits. The referral service can be reached at 800-FYI-CALL.

Finding Help

Many government and community agencies have websites. Many also provide excellent links to other sites that provide crime victims with information. Not all programs are on the Internet, but most nonprofit crime victim organizations obtain some state or federal funding in addition to private resources. Each state has an administrator for the federal funds, and this agency will have a listing of the programs that receive funding to provide crime victim assistance. Many private and public programs advertise or network with their local police or prosecutor, and they will be able to refer you to help.

If you have checked your local resources—police, prosecutors, the Yellow Pages, the library, city hall—and cannot find a local program, look for a statewide listing of victim service programs. Sometimes, a state agency or organization can provide assistance even if they are not based in your town or county. Contacting your attorney general's office can also be useful, since many of them have victim service information. Finally, your state representative or senator may have information to assist you in finding a local chapter of a statewide network.

No Local Programs

Some jurisdictions have not yet established formal programs to help victims. If you have no luck in finding a program, there may nonetheless be an informal group that meets. Ask your local police officer or prosecutor for assistance in finding such a group. In Appendix A of this book you will find selected national agencies that may also be able to assist you in finding a local resource.

Understanding Criminal Law | 3

Overview

The criminal justice system is designed to deter the commission of crimes, investigate and prosecute crimes, and punish and attempt to rehabilitate offenders. There is no single system. Instead, the phrase *criminal justice system* refers to a group of agencies that have the responsibility for taking action at certain times in a criminal case. The *police* take the report and investigate the crime. The *prosecutor* charges the accused and tries the case. The *judge* oversees the court process. *Corrections personnel* are responsible for the incarceration of the defendant. Each of these agencies is separate, and each has a different goal and purpose. Sometimes they do not work well together; however, in recent years, police and prosecutors have joined together to form task forces or specialized units to improve the handling of certain types of cases.

Criminal Law

There are federal laws and procedures that apply to cases prosecuted in the federal court system, but most crimes are prosecuted in the state court systems. Within constitutional limits, each state is free to enact its own criminal laws and procedural rules, and has the right to develop its own descriptions, definitions, and classification of crimes. For example, what is called *rape* in one state may be called *sexual battery* or *sexual assault* in another. In one state, it may be considered a single robbery if three people are held up at gunpoint while the attacker steals money from the cash register, but in another state it might be considered three robberies. The theft of $50 may be a misdemeanor in one state and a felony in another.

Types of Crimes

The most common classifications of crime in the United States are *misdemeanors* and *felonies*. Each state can determine which crimes are felonies and which are misdemeanors. One common method of categorizing crimes is by the length of sentence. The least serious crimes are called *petty offenses* or *infractions* in most states. Examples of typical petty offenses are:

- traffic violations;

- disturbing the peace; and,

- loitering.

In most states the maximum sentence for a misdemeanor is one year, although a few permit two years. Examples of typical misdemeanors are:

- assault;

- simple theft;

- trespassing;

- battery;

- public indecency (exposure); and,

- telephone harassment.

A felony is a more serious crime and can be punishable by longer prison terms, a life sentence, or even death. Examples of typical felonies are:

- murder;

- rape and sexual assault;

- arson;

- forgery;

- drugs (certain kinds);

- manslaughter;

- home invasion;

- carjacking;

- theft (over a certain amount); and,

- aggravated stalking.

Elements of Crimes

In order to constitute a crime, certain *elements* must be present. These will be stated in the actual laws.

EXAMPLE

A traditional first-degree murder requires proof of four elements:

1. killing a person;

2. unlawfulness (without a legally justifiable excuse, like self-defense);

3. intention; and,

4. malice aforethought (i.e., with prior planning).

If one or more of the elements is not present, it is not sufficient to charge the offense, although it may be possible to charge another lesser offense.

EXAMPLE

If the killing was *unlawful* (unauthorized) and *intentional* (not an accident), but *malice aforethought* (prior planning) was not present, it might still be charged as a lesser offense of second-degree murder.

Every crime has its own definition. An example of a criminal statute in Illinois defining the offense of residential burglary is: *A person commits residential burglary who knowingly and without authority enters the dwelling place of another with the intent to commit therein a felony or theft.*

The definition of *dwelling* is found in another section of Illinois' criminal code:

> *For the purposes of Section 19-3 of this Code, dwelling means a house, apartment, mobile home, trailer, or other living quarters in which, at the time of the alleged offense, the owners or occupants actually reside or in their absence intend within a reasonable period of time to reside.*

Thus in order to fully understand the required elements of an offense, you might need to research more than one statute or section of law.

The Offender

Once a person is accused of a crime, he or she becomes a party to the case and is entitled to the protection of the U.S. Constitution and all laws that apply to persons charged with a crime. Everyone who participates in committing the crime can be charged with the offense.

EXAMPLE

If three carjackers steal your car, each can be charged even if only one has the gun or drives away. The others can be held to be accountable for the actions of the gun-wielding driver.

An example of an *accountability statute* is:

Either before or during the commission of an offense, and with the intent to promote or facilitate such commission, he solicits, aids, abets, agrees, or attempts to aid such other person in the planning or commission of the offense.

Juveniles

Teenage and younger offenders are responsible for a large percentage of the crimes committed in the United States today. Until recently, however, juveniles who committed crimes were considered *delinquent* and sent to a special juvenile court for processing. Most state laws still only permit criminal convictions against older teen offenders on the theory that younger children are not fully responsible for their conduct. Some states do permit transfer to an adult court of a juvenile who commits a particularly violent or brutal crime.

Family Members

Family members can and do commit crimes against one another. Most often, the crimes of violence are called *domestic violence*, but family members commit a range of criminal acts against one another. Technically, the criminal law does not distinguish between a family member offender and a stranger, but in fact, the criminal justice system seems to treat crimes committed by family members as being less serious. For many years, the criminal justice system treated crimes between family members as private disputes and not public wrongs. Concepts of private family matters sometimes do affect charging decisions and sentencing options for family member offenders.

The State's Case

In our system of justice, a criminal defendant is always presumed innocent. Therefore, in all cases, the state has the entire burden of proving through the introduction of testimony or physical evidence at trial *beyond a reasonable doubt* that a crime was committed and that the defendant committed the crime. The defense has no *burden of proof* in a criminal case. (The defense does not even have to prove innocence.) The Fifth Amendment to the U.S. Constitution guarantees that the defendant cannot be made to *incriminate* (testify against) him- or herself. That is why the defendant does not have to testify.

In the majority of cases, the *testimony* of a single witness is legally sufficient to convict a defendant in a criminal case.

Even *circumstantial evidence* may be sufficient to convict a defendant. But because judges and juries want to have as much evidence as possible before convicting, often the state will introduce physical and scientific evidence in addition to the testimony of the victim and other witnesses.

Scientific evidence, such as DNA, is being used today in many cases. *DNA* is short for deoxyribonucleic acid; is found in saliva, blood, and other bodily fluids; and, can provide evidence that a person was at the crime scene.

The Defense's Case

When a *defendant* is charged with a crime, he or she may be entitled to an appointed attorney as guaranteed by the Sixth Amendment. In all cases, a defendant with the financial resources can hire an attorney. The defense attorney is present to ensure that a defendant's rights are not violated. The goal of the defense is to obtain a dismissal or acquittal whenever possible. The strategies used will vary depending on the kind of case, but will generally be as follows:

- the evidence is insufficient;

- the state violated the defendant's rights in gathering the evidence;

- the witnesses cannot be believed;

- consent or fabrication;

- mistaken identity;

- self-defense;

- entrapment or involuntary act; or,

- the defendant is unfit, insane, or guilty but mentally ill.

Insufficient Evidence

The defense may argue that the evidence is insufficient where there is little physical evidence, like fingerprints, to connect the defendant to the crime, and where the witnesses may have had little opportunity to observe the defendant.

Violated Rights

Even where there is strong physical evidence, like a match between the defendant's blood and blood collected at the scene, the defendant may argue that the state violated his or her rights in gathering the evidence. In this kind of case, the defense may also attack the police investigation techniques or the crime lab's processing and analyzing of the evidence.

Unbelievability

The defense may be that the victim cannot be believed. This defense is commonly seen where there are few witnesses other than the victim of the crime. The defendant attacks the motives of the victim in reporting the crime or in identifying the defendant.

EXAMPLE

The defendant might argue that the victim made up the story of the assault or battery to avoid getting into trouble for coming home late. Another defendant might claim that the victim wanted the insurance money for an item of property that was reported stolen.

Consent or Fabrication

In sexual assault cases where the defendant is an acquaintance of the victim, he may admit the sexual acts but contend that the victim agreed to have sex. This *consent* defense attacks the believability of the victim, and is often used where there is a lack of evidence of bruising or other injury to the victim. If the victim is a child, the defendant in this type of case will typically argue *fabrication* by the child due to immaturity or coaching by some adult.

Mistaken Identity

Mistaken identity is often claimed by defendants when the victim is physically injured or when the defendant is a stranger. This defense questions the victim's memory and accuracy of identification. Today, scientific improvements like fingerprinting and DNA genetic matching techniques have made it easier to identify stranger-defendants, but the mistaken identity defense is still raised where there is a lack of scientific evidence.

Self-Defense

In bodily harm, physical assault, or battery cases, the defendant may claim *self-defense*. Most states require the defendant to have acted on a reasonable belief that the conduct was necessary to avoid imminent physical harm or death, but the unreasonableness of a defendant's belief does not seem to deter claims of self-defense.

EXAMPLE

An Illinois newspaper reported that when a two-hundred-pound man was arrested for the murder of his one-hundred-and-ten-pound coworker, he claimed he stabbed her to death in self-defense after she tried to force him to have sex in the parking garage on their way to work.

Entrapment

A defendant may also claim *entrapment* as a defense. This is common in drug cases where the defendant contends that the police enticed or lured the defendant into committing the criminal acts. Another defense, *involuntariness*, might be seen in gang or multiple-offender cases where the defendant argues that he or she was forced by the other defendants to go along with and commit the crime.

Insanity

One of the required elements for a criminal charge is the ability to form a criminal intent. When a defendant is incapacitated, unfit, or insane, he or she may claim that he or she lacked the necessary mental state to commit the crime or to stand trial for committing the crime. All states have procedures for determining fitness and sanity. These hearings will require expert psychiatric evaluation and testimony, and may result in the deferral of prosecution for some period of time. If such an option is not available, there may be a finding of dangerousness or insanity, and a proceeding to commit the defendant into a mental health facility for treatment until he or she is no longer dangerous or insane. Such a defendant is then subject to release under the state's mental health code.

In some states, *guilty but mentally ill* is permitted as a method of responding to some of these criminals. A finding of guilty but mentally ill permits the state to incarcerate these offenders in mental health facilities for the duration of their mental illness, then transfer them to prison for the remainder of their sentences.

Temporary Insanity

Temporary insanity may be raised as a defense where a defendant claims that he or she was insane at the time the crime was committed and therefore should not be held responsible for it. The *twinkie defense*, in which the defendant claims that high levels of blood sugar caused the crime, and other diminished capacity defenses are similar type of claims. In these defenses, the defendant has recovered shortly after the crime, but still seeks to excuse his or her actions on the theory that he or she did not have the necessary criminal intent to commit the crime.

THE POLICE

Reporting the Crime

Reporting the crime to police sets the criminal justice system in motion. An immediate report to police provides the best opportunity to apprehend the offender before crucial evidence is lost or destroyed. Prompt reporting is also important for prosecution.

Some victims immediately report the crime. In other cases, a passerby, eyewitness, friend, or family member calls the police. Once you call the police, do not reenter or move about in the areas where the offender was present. These areas will become the *crime scene* and may produce evidence to convict the offender of the crime. If you have been physically injured, or if there is blood or other bodily fluids on (or in) you, resist the urge to wash up. Do not change your clothes. The hospital will want to collect these items as evidence. If you use a towel or other item to wipe the blood off, tell the police so that it can be collected.

Waiting to Report

In cases of violence between acquaintances, domestic violence, rape, and child abuse, it is not unusual for the victim to wait hours, days, months, or even years before notifying police. Although the police are primarily trained to investigate current reports of crime, many departments encourage citizens to report older cases as a way of solving repeat crimes. A criminal may continue to attack victims, developing a pattern over time, but police cannot begin to recognize it as a pattern unless victims report the crimes. Even if a victim waited several years to report, if the offender has continued to commit crimes, the victim's evidence may still be used in a criminal case to establish a pattern or for sentencing information in another current case. Today, DNA databases have identified many offenders in unsolved crimes. Some police departments have special *cold case units* that review old cases using advanced technology to iden-tify offenders.

The Role of Hospitals and Medical Personnel

If the victim does not report the crime to police but instead seeks treatment at a hospital or medical facility, in certain states the hospital is required by state law to notify the police. The victim may choose to proceed with charges or not, but the police will come to the hospital.

Hospitals are a part of the criminal justice system because they can collect evidence on the victim's body. For example, in a rape case, the hospital can collect hairs, fibers, semen, saliva, and blood left by the offender on the victim. In most states, this examination is free of charge, and some states have a standardized evidence collection kit. If the victim presses charges, the hospital gives the evidence directly to police.

Do not be afraid to ask medical personnel what the procedures and tests are that you are going through. Some hospitals have a crisis or social worker who can come to the emergency room to explain procedures. Others may call a crisis worker upon your request. You may not be able to understand everything, but it may help calm you to know what is happening.

If you have blood on your clothes, or other evidence of the crime, your clothes will be taken as evidence. In such a case, you will need a change of clothes. Sometimes, hospitals have sweatsuits or other clothing to give to the victim. If you are a family member or loved one, be sure to bring clothing for the victim to the hospital. It can often help to regain a sense of control to have your own clothing after the emergency medical treatment is finished.

The Police Investigation

Police are responsible for taking crime reports, investigating, collecting evidence, and apprehending suspects. Investigation includes questioning the victim and all witnesses to the crime, and identifying, collecting, and analyzing evidence to prove the existence of the crime. Any item of information that can be used to prove an element of the crime is considered evidence.

Upon arrival on the scene, the responding officer should begin by identifying him- or herself and determining what crime occurred. Police officers are now trained in *crisis intervention* techniques that are designed to increase their sensitivity to the stress of the victim. The officer will immediately determine whether emergency medical treatment is necessary and call for the appropriate assistance.

The Victim Interview

The officer will question the victim to obtain preliminary information, if the victim is able to be interviewed. The victim will be asked to described what happened (date, time, place, details) and to provide information concerning the defendant's identity or description. For example, the officer will want to know how the offender made contact with you. The offender may be following a pattern; he or she may be an experienced criminal who commits crimes only at certain times or in certain places.

Sometimes the offender will test the victim before a robbery, mugging, or other attack. This testing can be a brief conversation, like asking for help or directions. It is important, if possible, for you to recall the exact words that were used. What actions did the offender engage in? The offender may have a telltale nervous habit such as a twitch or muscle tic that can help identify him or her. During the attack, it is important to remember what the offender did, said, and touched.

Finally, did the offender threaten you by telling you not to call the police, or warn you that he or she knew where you lived or worked? Sometimes, an offender will boast about other crimes he or she has committed.

> ### EXAMPLE
>
> During a robbery, the robber might say, "Don't be like that other man and fight me." Police can use that information to try to link the offender with other area crimes with similar patterns.

Police recognize that the shock of the crime may cause a victim's initial statement to be confused or disorganized. If the officer asks clarifying questions, do not assume that he or she is challenging you or does not believe you. He or she simply may need more details. You may not know the answer to some of the questions or remember certain details. If you do not know or cannot remember, let the officer know that. Do not try to fill in the gaps with what you think or guess. At a follow-up interview you may remember more.

Police are also trained to understand that many victims may express their frustration and fears through anger, and may direct some of their anger at the officer. They do not usually take it personally.

After the responding officer has obtained preliminary information, the suspect's description will be broadcast to other officers in the area and a search for the offender will begin. The responding officer will continue to question any other witnesses to the crime.

The Crime Scene

The *crime scene* is a phrase used to describe any area of the crime in which evidence might be present that helps prove the crime. A crime scene can be a car, bedroom, house, business, section of the woods, trail, or any other place where the crime occurred. Police will immediately close off the crime scene so that no one except evidence technicians has access until all potential physical evidence is collected. If the crime scene is outside, it is very important that police immediately close the area to traffic so it does not become contaminated by people moving through it.

The crime scene may contain physical evidence such as fibers, hair, stains, finger-prints, or footprints. The victim can help police identify the crime scene area by pointing out how and where the offender came into contact with the victim, the movement of the offender, and what was touched during the crime. The victim can also identify what the offender took from the crime scene upon leaving. As previously noted, even the victim can be part of the crime scene if the attack was a personal assault.

Police will collect all items that may contain evidence and mark them for review by crime lab scientists. Crime laboratories exist in all states. The *Federal Bureau of Investigation* (FBI) also does crime analysis. The laboratory receives the evidence and scientifically analyzes it to determine what it is and where it may have come from.

EXAMPLE

In a case where the victim is murdered, fibers found on the victim's body may be identified as matching the carpet of a certain make and model of car. This evidence is then reported to the investigator on the case, who may be able to link that type of car with the defendant.

The Detective's Role

If the offender is known, the police will attempt to locate and question that person. If the victim or witnesses do not know the identity of the offender, and the suspect is not immediately found from the description given, a report is completed and the case is usually turned over to a detective or investigator for follow-up.

In larger departments, the detective or investigator continues the investigation into the facts of the crime. This officer is usually more experienced than the patrol or responding officer, and will follow up all leads in an effort to identify and collect evidence. The detective will likely need to reinterview the victim. This time, the interview will be in much greater detail in an effort to uncover additional information that might help in the investigation. If the suspect is unknown, the detective may investigate possible candidates for motives and alibis.

The Rights of the Victim

Under victims' rights laws, the victim has a right in many states to information on the status of the investigation, and where it does not compromise the investigation, the police will usually provide that information. Although it is the practice of many police officers to routinely keep the victim informed, the law may require that the victim request such information. In any event, it is a good idea to write a letter to the detective or investigator requesting to be kept informed of the status of the investigation. (see form 1, p.159.)

Address the request to the police officer in charge of the investigation, usually called an *investigator* or *detective*. Usually this is the officer who will maintain contact with you to provide updates and information as the case progresses, but sometimes a victim must contact the police station to find out who has been assigned to the case. Once the name of the investigator is available, do not be afraid to call that person and ask about the case. This keeps the case on the mind of an investigator who may have several ongoing cases. After the interviews, periodically ask to meet with the investigator to talk about your case.

Because you will have a lot of unfamiliar feelings and questions, it might help if you keep a log and write down your questions and the names of the persons you have spoken to in the police department concerning your case. Also, if you remember additional details, you should write these down and contact the police promptly with this information. You may be unaware that you possess vital information, or you may remember something that the police do not know.

Arrest of the Offender

Identifying the Offender

The police have a variety of methods to track down the identity of possible suspects. If the suspect is caught near the scene shortly after the crime, and the victim is able to, the victim may be asked to identify the offender in a procedure called a *showup*. In a showup, the suspect is shown to the victim for identification purposes. A showup may be at the scene or at the police station, or the victim may be taken to the suspect by police car.

A victim may also go to the police station to look through a series of *mug book* pictures of prior offenders or to help an artist make a composite drawing in an effort to identify the suspect. Or the victim may go to the police station to attend a *lineup* procedure.

Lineup Procedures. Lineups can be in-person or by photos. Many victims fear in-person lineups because they think the offender can see them. In an in-person lineup, several persons matching the same general description are literally lined up with the suspect. The victim views the suspects through a one-way mirror or with some other device that permits the victim to see the individuals, while they cannot see the victim. If the suspect has been charged with a crime, he or she has a right to have an attorney present. The suspect's attorney will be permitted to observe you as you examine the lineup participants.

The police detective should first explain the procedures involved in the lineup, and keep you out of sight of the offender. Do not hesitate to ask the officer to stay near you during the identification procedure if you feel concerned. The officer will ask you if you recognize any of the individuals, and if so, how you know them. Take your time in looking at the lineup, and if you can identify the offender, do so clearly. This establishes the identification of the defendant as the offender without any prompting from the police.

In smaller jurisdictions where an in-person lineup is not feasible, a photo lineup may be used. Several photos depicting similar-looking individuals are shown to the victim. The victim is then asked the same questions as in the in-person lineup procedure.

Unknown Offenders

If the victim does not know the identity of the offender and cannot identify him or her in the mug books, the police may use new scientific advances in an effort to identify the attacker. For example, DNA can positively identify a person by his or her genes because every person's DNA is unique. If the offender leaves his or her DNA at the scene through blood, saliva, or semen, the police can collect it and send it to a crime lab for identification.

Making the Arrest

Once sufficient information is available, if the offender can be found, police should arrest the suspect. Upon arrest, the defendant will be read his or her *Miranda rights* to remain silent and to obtain an attorney. If the defendant chooses not to talk to police, the police cannot continue to question him or her. If the defendant chooses to talk, any statement the defendant gives to police will be closely scrutinized later to determine whether the defendant's rights were violated and whether the statement was given voluntarily.

After the arrest, police continue to gather evidence to meet the legal elements of the case.

EXAMPLE

Upon arrest, the offender's clothes and body are examined for possible evidence. The police will take his or her clothes as potential evidence. Photographs of the offender may be taken to show any identifying marks or defensive wounds the victim may have inflicted.

The police will continue to search for any property taken from the victim. For example, if the charge is based on a home invasion in which several items were stolen, the police will search for and try to recover any of the stolen property to be used as evidence in the case. All persons have a right against unreasonable search and seizure, and the police may be required to obtain search warrants from a judge in order to collect some of the evidence.

What if Police Do Not Make an Arrest?

In any number of cases, police may not arrest a suspect. There may be insufficient evidence of all the legally required elements of the crime, or the offender may never be identified. If police do have sufficient evidence, the offender may have fled the jurisdiction or gone into hiding to evade arrest. If the police do not make an arrest once the suspect is known or his or her whereabouts are known, the victim can request that the police continue the investigation as new information is uncovered. The victim should also ask to meet with the investigator to find out why an arrest has not been made. If the victim is not able to meet with the investigator, he or she should ask to meet with the chief of detectives, a captain, or even the chief of police for an explanation. If the police will not arrest the suspect, the victim can go to the local prosecutor's office or the attorney general's office and seek assistance.

CHARGING THE CRIME   5

Who Can File Charges

Because the government must prosecute a criminal case, the final decision to pursue a state charge rests with a county or city prosecutor (also known by other names such as a *district attorney*, *parish prosecutor*, *borough prosecutor*, or *state's attorney*). For federal charges, the decision rests with the U.S. Attorney's Office. For felony cases, once police have completed their investigation, the police file and all reports are provided to the prosecutor's office for consideration. In some jurisdictions, for misdemeanor cases, police may recommend that charges be filed or may file a charge if a police officer witnessed the offense. Similarly, the victim may also pursue a misdemeanor charge against a defendant by appearing before a court officer and requesting a charge be filed. In all cases, the prosecutor represents the government.

Deciding What to Charge

Prosecutors have a great deal of discretion in deciding what to charge, and the law may permit the prosecutor to choose from several different possible charges. For example, a prosecutor may choose to file a less serious misdemeanor rather than a felony in a given case. The prosecutor may also choose not to file a charge at all, usually based on one or more of the following reasons:

- reasonable doubt of the suspect's guilt;
- reluctance of a key witness to testify;

- cooperation of the accused in the arrest of others;

- a legal element of the case is not present; or,

- the circumstances of the crime are such that a jury is unlikely to convict.

If a decision is made not to prosecute, some larger prosecutor's offices have established a review process, sometimes called *felony review*. If you believe the prosecutor assigned to your case did not have all the evidence or failed to consider a crucial piece of information, a review should be requested and the prosecutor should reconsider filing charges in light of the additional evidence. If the prosecutor still refuses to charge, consider contacting the head of the prosecutor's office or your state's attorney general for assistance.

Methods of Charging

There are generally three methods by which a crime can be charged—*complaint*, *information*, and *indictment*. In some jurisdictions, petty offenses and less serious misdemeanors are charged by a *complaint form*. This complaint may be made by the victim or the prosecutor on a form provided by the county or municipal criminal court clerk's office.

For felony crimes, the prosecutor signs the complaint, which may be called an *information*. The case then goes before a judge at a preliminary hearing to determine whether there is sufficient evidence to proceed with bringing the defendant to trial. The prosecutor can also take the case before a grand jury to seek an *indictment*. In some states, even if the grand jury refuses to indict, the prosecutor can still file a complaint.

The Grand Jury

The *grand jury* process may be used instead of the preliminary hearing (see Chapter 6 for an explanation of preliminary hearings) or in addition to a preliminary hearing. A grand jury is like any other jury. It is made up of citizens usually selected from the voter or motor vehicle registration lists. The grand jury determines whether charges should proceed in criminal cases brought before it.

The prosecutor presents evidence to the grand jury that will determine whether there is probable cause to charge the defendant. If the grand jury believes there is probable cause, it renders a *true bill*. If not, it renders *no bill*. (Generally, the grand jury will render a true bill because only the prosecutor presents evidence at the grand jury hearing. Therefore, the grand jury usually does not hear any evidence that tends to indicate the defendant is not guilty.) If a true bill is returned, the defendant is indicted and a warrant will be issued for his or her arrest. If no bill is returned, the case does not go forward. If the defendant has already been picked up, he or she is released.

Time Limits

With the exception of murder, nearly all offenses have time limits within which the charges must be filed against the suspect. There are exceptions to the time limits, and each state varies in the limitation period it permits for charging crimes. These time limits are called *statutes of limitation*, since they literally limit the time within which a charge can be brought. Even if the offense has a time limit, there are exceptions to the statutes of limitation.

EXAMPLE

If the suspect flees the jurisdiction before he or she can be arrested, the time period stops while the suspect is absent from the state.

Special Cases

Many states have also extended the time period for cases in which the victim is a child and for some types of sex offenses. These crimes cause serious trauma that may keep a victim from reporting the crime to authorities for a long period of time. It may be only after the victim becomes an adult that the crime can be safely reported to police. A number of states have extended the time limit for charging this kind of case.

The Charges in Your Case

To fully understand what crimes are charged in your case, obtain the exact statutory citation, which will be listed on the charges filed against the defendant. Ask your prosecutor or victim-witness coordinator to provide you with a copy of the charges. With these statutory section numbers, you can find the state's criminal code, which will list the elements and the potential sentences for each crime. (See Appendix C on legal research.)

PRETRIAL PROCEDURES 6

The procedures before trial often determine the strength of the prosecution's and defense's cases, and will narrow the issues to be raised at the trial. This is the longest part of the criminal case and can take more than a year to complete. It can be very difficult to wait that long for a resolution of the case, and in some jurisdictions there have been efforts to speed up the process. Nevertheless, the defendant often benefits by extending the time, hoping the victim will give up or witnesses may move away and the case will be harder to prove with the passage of time.

The Victim's Right to Notice and to Protection

In most states, the victim has the right to know what the status of the case is prior to trial. In some states, prosecutors will automatically notify the victims of pending dates, but if your state requires that you request this information, be sure to put your request in writing. For a sample letter to the prosecutor, see form 2 in Appendix E (p.160).

Victims are entitled to be free from intimidation and harassment while attending court proceedings. A secure or safe waiting area may mean a separate waiting room, or waiting in the office of the prosecutor or the victim-witness coordinator, or it may mean waiting in an empty jury room or office. If no provisions have been made in advance, ask the prosecutor for assistance in directing you to a waiting area that eliminates your contact with the defendant, his or her family, and his or her friends while awaiting hearings. If you or your family are harassed, threatened, or harmed at any time during the criminal proceedings, immediately notify police and the prosecutor so that appropriate action can be taken to protect you or your family.

Speedy Trial

The defendant has a right to a speedy trial, which is defined by law. The time period is shorter if the defendant remains in jail pending trial. The defendant can demand that the state meet the time limits and if it fails, the case will be dismissed and the defendant released. If the state violates the defendant's speedy trial rights, the defendant cannot be retried because it would violate the U.S. Constitution. However, in many cases when the defendant requests a continuance, he or she is required to waive his or her right to a speedy trial, at least for the period of the delay he or she seeks.

Some states have provided that the victim has a right to a *speedy disposition*. This right is not accorded the same weight as the defendant's rights, but it may entitle the victim to object to delay, or the prosecutor to raise the effect of continuances on victims. Some judges are becoming more sensitive to the needs of victims in determining whether to grant continuances. Violation of a victim's right to a speedy disposition will not result in dismissal or release of the defendant.

Arraignment—Defendant's Initial Appearance

Within a short time after arrest, the accused, now called the *defendant*, is brought before a judge for the initial appearance, called an *arraignment*. The arraignment proceeding informs the defendant of the charges and provides an opportunity for the defendant to make a *plea* of guilty, not guilty, or no contest.

If the defendant pleads *guilty*, he or she admits the charges and a conviction can be entered against him or her. A *not guilty* plea means that the case will continue toward trial. In a *no contest* or *nolo contendere* plea, the defendant does not admit anything and agrees that the court may enter a conviction against him or her (*nolo contendere* means "I will not contest"). A no contest plea is helpful for the defendant because the facts of the case are not proven and thus cannot be used in a later civil trial as evidence of guilt. If the defendant does not answer or make a plea, it will be presumed that the plea is not guilty.

At this first hearing, an attorney will be appointed for the defendant if he or she cannot afford his or her own attorney. The defendant has a right to have the charges read, but many defendants waive this right. The defendant will likely plead not guilty. Where bail has not been preset, the judge makes the decision to grant or deny bail to the defendant. The date for the next hearing, usually called a *preliminary hearing*, will most likely be scheduled at this time.

Bail

Most defendants are eligible for release pending trial. *Bail* is the method by which a defendant provides money or other security to ensure his or her return to court. The *bond* is the document the defendant signs that identifies what was posted (e.g., money, house, etc.) as his or her security. In the least serious cases, pretrial release is permitted without bail, and bail is generally available to most defendants who are charged with a crime. Exceptions differ by state law, but generally certain types of murder charges are *nonbailable offenses*. Originally, the purpose of bail was to ensure that the defendant would return to court for the trial, and the amount was set high enough to secure the defendant's return while not being excessive, which would violate his or her constitutional rights. Today, in addition to securing the defendant's appearance for trial, the protection of the victim and the public is also a consideration in setting bail.

The Bail Hearing

The amount of bail is preset for some crimes, so the defendant will know exactly how much he or she has to produce to gain release. If the defendant can produce bail, he or she can be released within a short time after the arrest. Many victims are shocked to see the defendant out on the street the day after being arrested.

In serious felonies, bail is not usually preset, and a bail hearing will be held to determine the amount and conditions of bail. In a bail hearing, the court will consider:

- the nature and circumstances of the crime, including whether there was force, weapons, impact on, and injuries to the victim;

- the likelihood that the prosecution may upgrade the charge to a more serious offense;

- the defendant's attempts, if any, to avoid prosecution;

- the defendant's ties to the community;

- the defendant's prior criminal history;

- the potential sentence for the offense charged; and,

- relevant victim information.

Today, the prosecutor can present evidence of the defendant's dangerousness, and the judge will consider whether the defendant is a threat to the victim, the victim's family, or the public in deciding whether to grant bail. In California, for example, the protection of the public is a primary concern in bail consideration.

Generalized fear of the defendant will not usually be a sufficient reason to deny bail, but the presence of threats by the defendant during the crime or the actions of the defendant's family or friends in intimidating the victim should be brought to the prosecutor's attention prior to any hearing on bail so that the judge can take that into consideration when determining whether to grant bail. If the defendant has made threats against you or you have reason to fear that the defendant knows where you work or live, ask your prosecutor to request the judge to deny bail to the defendant.

If the defendant is granted bail, he or she must usually put up a bond. In rare cases, the *bond* is the defendant's word that he or she will return. The defendant who is permitted to sign for his or her release is said to be released on his or her own *recognizance*.

More likely, the defendant will have to post a monetary bond. The exact amount of the bond depends on state law, but it may be some percentage of the total amount, and it can be deposited in money, property, or another item of value. Some jurisdictions permit a defendant to post a percentage of the court-ordered bail amount. The court is entitled to an administration fee and will return the deposit if the defendant meets the conditions of bond. If the defendant does not, the full court-ordered amount is forfeited.

Bail is usually higher in felonies because of the seriousness of the crime. If the defendant cannot deposit the amount required, or if bail is denied, the defendant will remain in jail while awaiting trial.

Conditions of Bail

If the defendant is out on bail pending trial, every state has certain conditions that must be met, and additional conditions that can be required by the judge for the defendant to remain free.

Mandatory conditions commonly include that the defendant:

- appear at all court dates;

- follow all court orders;

- remain in the state pending trial; and,

- commit no crimes pending trial.

If the prosecutor produces evidence that other conditions are necessary to protect the victim, the victim's family, or the public before trial, the court can include other items, such as that the defendant:

- possess no firearms;

- refrain from communicating to the victim or the victim's family;

- refrain from following the victim or appearing at the victim's school or work;

- refrain from alcohol or drug use;

- undergo alcohol or drug treatment;

- undergo counseling;

- get or keep a job;

- attend school;

- support his or her dependents;

- observe a curfew;

- remain in the custody of another person or agency;

- be supervised by another person or agency; and,

- vacate the household (if the victim is a family member).

In Utah, the victim has a right to appear before the judge to provide input on issues related to the defendant's release. In most states, however, the prosecutor is charged with presenting evidence on dangerousness, so make sure to tell the prosecutor before the hearing to include as a condition of bail that the defendant stay away from your work, home, and family.

Get a copy of the court order listing the conditions of the defendant's pretrial release. If you believe the defendant has violated any of the conditions, tell the prosecutor right away. Call the police if the violation is immediate, so you can get help and the violation can be recorded. When the defendant violates conditions of pretrial release, he or she can lose the right to freedom while awaiting trial.

Preliminary Hearing

The *preliminary hearing* is usually held soon after the defendant's initial court appearance. The purpose of this hearing is to determine whether probable cause exists that a crime was committed and that this defendant committed the crime. This hearing will be held before the judge. The police officer will testify and the victim may also be called as a witness.

The defendant does not have to produce any witnesses since he or she has no burden of proving his or her case, but the defendant does have the right to cross-examine any prosecution witness at this hearing. After the witnesses have been presented, the judge will either determine that there is sufficient evidence to continue to trial, or dismiss the case and release the defendant.

Pretrial Motions

Most criminal court cases are delayed for a considerable time period while the state and defendant investigate the case. Both the state and the defendant may request information and may file *motions* to discover information. Motions are merely oral or written requests made to a judge. Motions can involve the charges, witnesses, or evidence. Many motions will not require the victim's presence, such as motions directed at the legal validity of the charges or motions to admit other crimes' evidence. Even so, in some states, notice of scheduled hearings on these motions may be provided to victims. Some common motions include:

- motion to dismiss;

- motion to suppress;

- motion for continuance;

- motion for change of judge or venue; and,

- motion for discovery.

Motion to Dismiss

A motion to dismiss can be made by the state or defendant. Sometimes the state will elect to proceed on a few of many possible charges, and so may dismiss the rest at some point prior to trial. The defendant may also ask the court to dismiss the case on the basis that the charge is defective because it fails to meet the legal requirements. A defendant may also ask the court to dismiss the case when the state failed to meet his or her speedy trial rights.

Motion to Suppress

The defendant may make a motion to suppress the introduction of evidence of his or her arrest or identification by the victim. This motion is also made by the defendant to stop the state from using a confession or other evidence obtained in violation of the defendant's rights. For example, the defendant may argue that the confession was not voluntary, that he or she was denied the right to legal counsel, or that items were taken from him or her in an unreasonable search or seizure. If such a motion is granted by the judge, the state would not be able to use that confession or item of evidence against the defendant at trial. Hopefully, the other evidence against the defendant will be sufficient for a conviction.

Motion for Continuance

Trials may be continued for legitimate reasons, like a delay in analyzing evidence or witness unavailability, but many cases are continued at the request of the defendant as a strategy to make the victim drop out of the case. Judges are trained to scrutinize the reasons for continuance requests. In some states, special consideration must be given to the effect of a continuance on the victim.

EXAMPLE

In Ohio, the victim can object to a substantial delay in proceedings, and upon request, the prosecutor will file a motion with the court to consider the victim's wishes.

Motion for Change of Judge or Venue

If the judge is prejudiced, or if, for example, pretrial publicity is so biased that the defendant cannot get a fair trial, these motions may be filed seeking to change the judge or move the trial.

Motion for Discovery

These very common motions are often searches for evidence. Most motions relate to the identification, analysis, or production of forensic or scientific evidence. Some motions may involve questions surrounding the identification and qualification of expert witnesses.

With regard to discovering information concerning the victim, states apply differing approaches. Victims may generally refuse to speak to, or to be interviewed by, the defendant or defense investigators. In some states, however, the victim may be required or ordered to attend a deposition to give a statement before a court reporter under oath. In others, depositions are not permitted in criminal court. To protect its victims, an Arizona constitutional amendment provides that victims may refuse interviews, depositions, or other discovery requests.

Plea Bargaining

7

Plea bargaining has existed in some form in the United States since the early 1800s. Today, it is not unusual for some jurisdictions to resolve 80–90% of their felony cases by plea bargain. It is called a *bargain* because both the state and the defendant derive some benefit from the deal. The state does not have to risk a trial and the possibility of losing (and the defendant gets at least some punishment and a criminal record), and the defendant does not have to risk a longer or more severe sentence. The judge must still approve of the agreement before it can be entered in the court. A judge can also reject a plea bargain.

Because of the critical impact that a plea bargain has on the victim, states now permit or require prosecutors to confer or consult with victims before an agreement is made. Several states require prosecutors to consider the victim's concerns prior to engaging in plea negotiations. At least one state (Maine) requires the prosecutor to state the victim's wishes in court before an agreement is approved by a judge.

To include victim impact information, some states require the victim to prepare a victim impact statement. See the section in Chapter 9 on "The Victim Impact Statement" for details on what should be included in such a statement.

Types of Plea Bargains

There are two major types of plea bargains. In the first type, the defendant negotiates away certain charges so that only a lesser charge (or charges) remains pending.

EXAMPLE

If a defendant is facing two charges—a home invasion with a possible sentence of six to thirty years and burglary with a possible sentence of three to seven years—by pleading guilty to the burglary in exchange for dismissing the home invasion, the defendant has reduced his potential sentence to a maximum of seven years (instead of thirty).

The second type involves an agreement by the state and defendant to a particular sentence in exchange for a guilty plea. In the previous example, the state and defendant would agree that the prosecutor would ask for no more than fifteen years on the home invasion (rather than the thirty possible), and three years on the burglary (rather than seven).

Rarely the defendant enters into a third type of plea, called an *open plea*, in which the judge decides the sentence without negotiation.

Procedures

Plea negotiations most often take place very early in a case. In this way, the defendant tests the confidence of the prosecutor to see how strong the state thinks its case is, or the state may test the defendant to see how readily the case can be disposed. For example, if the prosecutor feels the evidence is weak or a victim is wavering, the state may readily agree to a plea bargain.

Similarly, if the defendant is not confident of his or her ability to win at trial, but can arrange a lesser sentence or a reduced charge, the defendant may be willing to plead guilty. The earlier the offer, the more likely it will be generous, but a plea bargain may be reached at any time, even in the middle of the trial.

The defendant has certain constitutional rights in making a plea, and his or her plea must be voluntary. Therefore, even if the judge approves of the agreement, there will be a short hearing before a court reporter in which the defendant will be questioned as to his or her understanding of the plea. It is critical that there be ongoing communication with the prosecutor in your case so that your views and victim impact information is put before the judge in determining whether to accept the plea.

CRIMINAL TRIAL

8

The Process of a Criminal Trial

If the defendant does not plead guilty, the case will go to trial. A *judge* presides over the criminal case. Today, most judges are attorneys with experience in criminal trials. When a legal question arises, the judge makes the decision based on the laws, procedures, and previous case decisions. He or she has a duty to remain impartial and to see that the criminal justice process is fair and just for all participants. This means that the judge should not take sides.

If a *jury* has been requested, the judge oversees the selection of the jury to be sure that a jury of the defendant's peers is chosen. The judge will determine whether the state has enough evidence to proceed with trial, and the judge is also the person who approves continuances. Once a jury is chosen, the judge will determine what evidence can be heard, subject to the applicable criminal law and rules of procedure. If a jury has not been requested, the trial is called a *bench trial* and the judge will decide both questions of law and fact.

All states have rules of evidence and procedure that govern the prosecution's and defense's questioning of the victim and other witnesses. If one side objects to a question, it is the judge who will decide whether the witness must answer the question.

The Victim's Rights to be Present

In many states, the victims' rights laws permit the victim to be present at court proceedings, subject to the rules of evidence, on the same basis as the defendant or at the judge's discretion. The rules of evidence govern whether a witness can be present in court. For example, courts often allow a prosecutor or defense motion to exclude witnesses where one witness's testimony might be improperly influenced by watching another witness testify.

If the defense tries to have you excluded from the proceedings, make an oral or written request to the prosecutor to permit you to stay in the courtroom. Unless the defense can show a valid reason why you should be kept out, you should be able to stay.

Also, some states permit you to have a support person present in court. The same objection should be made if the defense tries to keep out that person. The judge will make the final decision on whether you can be present and under what circumstances.

The Defendant's Right to a Jury

The trial may be by jury in serious criminal cases. Sometimes, it is the defendant's strategy to demand a jury, because in most states the verdict of the jury must be unanimous to convict. If the defendant can convince even one juror not to vote for conviction, then no guilty verdict will be entered against him or her.

Each state has adopted procedures for jury selection. Random pools of jurors are picked to appear and answer the questions of a judge or the attorneys in a questioning process called *voir dire* (pronounced "vwa dear"). The questions determine whether a proposed juror is qualified to serve on a particular jury and identify grounds for removal. Once a jury has been selected, the trial is ready to begin.

Opening Statements

The trial begins with an overview of the case, called an *opening statement*, given by each party or their attorney. The state has the entire burden of proving the case, so it goes first. The prosecutor outlines the theory of the case and what he or she believes the witnesses and any other evidence will prove to the jury (or to the judge in a bench trial).

The defense also has the right to make an opening statement, which will sometimes be given right after the prosecutor's opening statement and sometimes be given just before the defense attorney begins presenting his or her evidence. The defense attorney may wish to delay his or her opening statement until the prosecution has finished presenting all its evidence. This is because it may be difficult for the defense attorney to decide what witnesses he or she will call until he or she has heard and seen the prosecution's evidence.

If the defense believes that the prosecution has not presented a strong case, the defense attorney may decide that he or she does not need to present any testimony (since the prosecutor has the burden of proof, and the defendant is innocent until proven guilty beyond a reasonable doubt and cannot be required to testify).

Evidence and Testimony

All the information that can be considered by a judge or jury in a criminal trial is presented through witness testimony and by introducing documents, physical items, and scientific evidence. Each state has rules that govern the admissibility of evidence, and not all information that is relevant will be permitted to be introduced into the trial. For example, information that is highly prejudicial to the defendant, like a long-past criminal conviction, is weighed against its importance to the current case before it can be admitted.

One notable exception is California, which constitutionally provides for *truth in evidence* in criminal trials. California's Constitution provides that "relevant evidence shall not be excluded" in juvenile or criminal offenses except under specified circumstances. (Ca. Const. Article (Art.) I, Sec. 28(d).)

Most of the preliminary motions determine what evidence will be permitted at trial, but some questions may arise during trial. Objections may be raised by either the state or the defendant for many reasons. The judge must then decide the matter before the trial continues.

Each side will present witnesses by direct examination. The questions will be asked first by the attorney who is sponsoring the witness, followed by cross-examination by the opposing attorney.

EXAMPLE

A prosecution witness might be the police officer. The prosecutor asks questions on direct examination of the officer, which is followed by cross-examination by the defense.

Direct Examination

The purpose of *direct examination* is to have the witness tell the story to find out what happened, so the questions will be open-ended and allow the witness to explain the event. An example follows:

PROSECUTOR:	State your name and occupation.
POLICE OFFICER:	John Doe. I am a police officer with the Gotham City Police Department.
PROSECUTOR:	Do you recall the night of January 1, 2008?
POLICE OFFICER:	Yes.
PROSECUTOR:	Tell the court what happened that night.
POLICE OFFICER:	I was on duty that night, and at approximately 12:10 a.m., while driving my patrol car at the corner of Elm and Fifth Street, I observed a woman on the curb waving her arm at me.

Cross-Examination

The purpose of cross-examination is to limit or test the witness's recollection of the event, or to show that the witness has not told the entire story or is lying, in an attempt to undermine his or her credibility and reduce the impact of his or her testimony in the case. Cross-examination can also be used to show the bias, interest, or motive of the witness. The questions are designed to lead the witness to a particular answer.

Police are often attacked in a criminal case by the defense as a strategy to undermine the evidence against the defendant. The defense attorney in the previous example has checked the police roster for January 2 and found that the police officer was not on duty that day. He also noticed that the date on the officer's police report is January 6.

This led to the following exchange on cross-examination:

DEFENSE ATTORNEY: Isn't it a fact that you were *not* on duty that night?

POLICE OFFICER: No. I was on duty until 11:55 p.m., and was on my way home in my patrol car when I first saw Ms. Smith.

DEFENSE ATTORNEY: Isn't it true that you didn't even complete your police report until several days later?

POLICE OFFICER: Yes. I didn't complete my report until I could speak with a particular witness again.

DEFENSE ATTORNEY: So you don't really remember that night, do you?

POLICE OFFICER: I remember that night very clearly.

Here, the defense attorney's attempt to discredit the officer was not very successful, but you should get the idea of the difference between the tone of direct examination and cross-examination.

The State's Case

Because the state goes first, it chooses the order in which the state's witnesses will testify. Depending on the type of case, and an evaluation of available evidence, the prosecutor may have the victim testify first, but may also call other witnesses to set the stage for the victim's later testimony. Typical witnesses include police officers who investigated the case, evidence and lab technicians who collected and analyzed the evidence, eyewitnesses, and experts who can assist the judge or jury in understanding the evidence to be presented.

The Victim as a Witness

Preparation for Court

The victim may be the state's primary witness in the case and will usually be required to testify at trial. You have likely waited a long time for this day. Now that it has come, you are likely to be nervous and maybe frightened. You may have experienced testifying at the preliminary hearing or at some other pretrial motion, but that was some time ago.

The emotions experienced during the crime can be rekindled at the court hearings. For example, anger, fear, and hatred may interfere with your ability to tell the story. Today, you will be confronting the offender in court. The defendant's family and friends may also be in the courtroom watching you. The best way to overcome these fears is to be prepared.

Preparation by the prosecutor will help you, but you should also make an attempt to familiarize yourself with court procedures. If possible, make a visit to other courtrooms to watch testimony in unrelated cases. Sometimes victim-witness personnel in the prosecutor's office can set up a time for you to tour the courtroom in which you will likely testify. Even televised courtroom documentary programs may help you visualize the court process. Watch carefully the demeanor of the witnesses who testify, and especially become aware of the role of the defense attorney and of the strategies used in defending cases.

You should also know that it is perfectly proper to speak to the prosecutor before trial. The prosecutor will not tell you how to answer the questions, but he or she can help you work through your concerns about testifying. So if the defense attorney asks you on cross-examination or in a deposition if you have spoken to the prosecutor before trial, you can answer, "Yes," and when the defense attorney asks what the prosecutor told you to say, you can truthfully answer, "To tell the truth."

Testifying in Court

A victim's demeanor in testifying is very important. Sometimes, in an effort to be calm and controlled, the jury may think the victim is too unemotional to be genuine. And if the victim is too relaxed, the defense attorney may use that fact against him or her.

In preparing you to testify, the prosecutor will likely suggest that you:

- tell the truth;

- do not volunteer information;

- do not use drugs or alcohol to calm nerves;

- do not memorize testimony;

- be straightforward and speak clearly;

- say so, if you are unsure of the question;

- look at the judge or jury when answering a question;

- listen carefully to each question before answering;

- dress conservatively;

- understand that the goal of the defense attorney is to discredit you;

- if a question cannot be answered with a yes or no, say so, or explain that you must give two answers to the two-part question;

- do not guess at answering—if you do not know the answer, say, "I don't know";

- if you are interrupted before you finish your answer, ask if you can finish your first answer to the first question before answering a new question;

- if someone objects, stop talking and wait for the judge to rule;

- do not follow the commands or instructions of the defense attorney—only the judge can issue orders;

- do not argue with the defense attorney; and,

- control your anger.

If it seems like that is a lot to remember, that is because it is. But just do your best. You know what happened, so tell it as best you can to the judge and jury. You are not in control of all the rules and procedures, but you are in control of yourself.

The Defense's Case

After the state completes its case, the defendant is entitled to introduce his or her evidence using the same methods. The defendant may introduce alibi witnesses or witnesses who attack the evidence offered by the state. In criminal cases, however, the defendant has a constitutional right not to testify, and the state may not suggest any reason for the defendant's failure to testify. The state has the same right as the defendant to cross-examine the defense witnesses.

Closing Statements

After each side has completed its case, the state and defendant summarize their cases through closing arguments. The state will argue that the case has been proved beyond a reasonable doubt and will likely remind the judge or jury of each important witnesses' testimony. The defendant will argue that the state failed to prove that the defendant committed the crime beyond a reasonable doubt.

The defendant may also attack the state's witnesses, including you, as being unreliable or having a motive to lie, and therefore suggest that the evidence was false or improperly used against him or her. Once the defendant completes his or her closing argument, the state will usually have one more chance to convince the judge or jury that the evidence was sufficient to convict the defendant.

Findings and Verdicts

If it has been a bench trial, the judge will make the findings. If it has been a jury trial, the case moves to deliberation on a jury verdict. There are a range of possible verdicts in most states, including guilty, guilty but mentally ill, not guilty, and not guilty by reason of insanity. Contrary to what you may hear from members of the news media, innocent is not available as either a plea or a verdict.

If a judge or jury determines that the state did not prove guilt, the defendant is freed. A guilty verdict, on the other hand, means the defendant is guilty of one or more of the charges.

Insanity

Not guilty by reason of insanity developed from the concept that the law should not hold a person criminally accountable for actions over which he or she has no control. If a person lacks the ability to control his or her actions due to mental illness, then he or she is not to be blamed and should not be punished for his or her actions.

States differ on the standards and degrees to which the defense of insanity will be permitted. A person found not guilty by reason of insanity is usually released (unless someone begins a civil court proceeding to have him or her committed to a mental institution as being a danger to him- or herself or others).

Mental Illness

Because of public outrage over some defendants' attempts to use an insanity defense to get released, some states have adopted a verdict of *guilty but mentally ill*. If the jurors believe that the defendant did commit the illegal act, but has a mental illness, they may render a verdict of guilty but mentally ill. This verdict keeps the defendant in custody, and merely influences where he or she serves his or her sentence.

Upon conviction, the defendant undergoes a psychiatric evaluation to determine the nature and extent of his or her mental illness. Then the defendant is sent to a mental health facility to serve his or her sentence and receive treatment. If the defendant regains his or her mental health during the period of his or her sentence, he or she is transferred to prison for the remainder of the term.

Jury Instructions

In a jury trial, the judge instructs the jury on the law to be applied in its deliberation, and then the case goes to the jury. The jury's job is to determine whether the facts produced at trial fit the crimes charged against the defendant, and whether they believe beyond a reasonable doubt that the defendant committed the crimes charged. If the jury believes that the state has proved its case, then it will find the defendant guilty. In most states, the verdict must be unanimous, and this applies to both guilty and not guilty verdicts. Once the jury has reached a verdict, the judge will enter the judgment of conviction. Contrary to popular belief, most jury trials result in the conviction of the defendant on at least one charge.

Hung Jury

When a jury is unable to agree on a verdict, it is called a *hung jury* and the judge will declare a mistrial. The state will have another opportunity (if it chooses) to try the defendant again. If the jury agrees that the evidence presented did not prove beyond a reasonable doubt that the defendant is guilty, the jury can render a verdict of not guilty. In this case, the state cannot retry the defendant again, because to do so would violate the constitutional protection against *double jeopardy* (i.e., being tried twice for the same crime).

Verdict on Some Counts

The prosecutor may have charged several offenses for the acts committed by the defendant. The proof at trial may have convinced a jury that the defendant was guilty of only one or some of the charges, and a finding of guilt would be made on only those charges.

Sometimes the defendant is found guilty of a lesser included offense, which means that the defendant committed a crime but not the highest offense charged.

EXAMPLE

The defendant is charged with murder, which requires proving that the defendant: (1) killed the victim; and, (2) did so with the intent to cause death. The jury believes that the defendant did kill the victim, but that the defendant only intended to frighten the victim, not to kill him. Because the law requires both elements for a finding of guilt on the murder charge, but only one is present, the jury may find the defendant guilty of a lesser included offense such as *manslaughter* (defined as the unintentional killing of a person).

AFTER THE TRIAL

9

The Sentence

Sentencing generally serves three purposes—punishment, deterrence, and rehabilitation. Federal sentencing guidelines apply to federal cases, and each state has the right to design its sentencing scheme. States may follow an indeterminate sentencing scheme in which the judge sentences the defendant to a range of years, but the parole board may release the defendant after a certain period of time.

EXAMPLE

If the judge sentences a defendant to three years to life, the parole board can release the defendant upon a showing of rehabilitation even if the offender has not yet served the minimum length of time.

In a *determinate scheme*, the range of sentence is established by state law and the judge may sentence the defendant within that range. Parole is not available for defendants in a determinate sentencing scheme, so that a defendant would be sentenced for a set period, for example, ten years, and would be required by law to serve a minimum set portion of that sentence.

What the Sentence Really Means

Be aware that despite sentencing reforms around the country, often the prison sentence handed out by the judge is not exactly what the offender will actually serve. Over the years, time off for good behavior has become a standard, and an offender will usually serve only part of the actual sentence imposed if he or she behaves while in prison.

Another problem occurs when the offender is sent back to the community to a halfway house or with electronic home confinement. This prisoner may still be considered to be in custody even though he or she is back in the community, and you may be shocked because you were never notified.

Make sure that you have contact with the prosecutor after the sentence is imposed to get an explanation in clear terms as to what the sentence really means. Find out what office or department will monitor the defendant during the sentence. Get the name, telephone number, and address of the supervising official from the prosecutor. Many states specifically require that the victim be told what the true sentence term means in terms of years to be served.

Sentencing Dispositions

Every state has a specific sentencing code that sets forth the range of sentence dispositions for each crime. Some states permit the death penalty for certain types of murder; other states permit up to life in prison. Many states are adopting *truth in sentencing laws* that increase the time served by repeat offenders, and *three strikes and you're out laws*, which require life imprisonment for a career criminal upon the third conviction.

Most states permit a range of penalties for the same class of crime. For example, a home invasion and a criminal sexual assault may fall within the same offense classification, with the same potential sentencing range. Generally, the following dispositions exist (these are explained in more detail as follows):

- execution (in some states);

- imprisonment (including boot camp, periodic imprisonment, etc.);

- probation (possibly with home confinement, electronic monitoring, etc.);

- supervision;

- restitution; and,

- fines.

Execution

The most serious penalty available is the death penalty (*capital punishment*). A number of states permit this punishment after a conviction of its highest class of murder or murder with special circumstances.

Imprisonment

A jail or prison sentence may be mandatory for certain crimes. The maximum length of term is for the defendant's natural life, but some states provide for an *indefinite term* (one to one hundred years), while others require a *definite term* (299 years) to be imposed. Some states permit an extended term for exceptionally brutal or heinous behavior or for repeat offenders.

States may also permit or require sentences to be imposed *concurrently* (at the same time) or *consecutively* (one after the other) if necessary to protect the public. Offenders sentenced to prison will be in the custody of the state's department of corrections, which determines what prison the offender is sent to and whether the offender is transferred.

Boot camp. In recent years, boot camps have become popular for certain types of offenders. Boot camps are also called *impact incarceration*. They have eligibility requirements and many states exclude the most serious crimes or repeat offenders from the program. Boot camps usually last four to six months and require physical training and labor.

Periodic imprisonment. Periodic imprisonment means that the offender will be released during some portion of the sentence and will be confined during the remainder. For example, an offender might spend weekends in jail, but continue to work and support his or her family during the week. Or, a court may sentence the offender to spend one weekend per month in jail for the duration of the sentence imposed.

Probation

Crimes that include probation as an option tend to be less serious offenses. The possible length of probation varies with the crime charged. A sentence of *probation* means that the offender is convicted of the crime, but is permitted to remain in the community subject to certain conditions.

Probation may also include some term of periodic imprisonment or community service as part of the sentence. Even if the crime permits probation, a judge can refuse to grant it if he or she believes that the crime charged requires some length of incarceration.

Conditions of probation usually include that the offender:

- not commit any crime;

- report to a probation officer;

- not possess a dangerous weapon;

- not leave the state without the court's permissions; and,

- not associate with other convicted people.

In addition, the court can impose other conditions on the offender, and some states require a court to impose certain conditions based on the offense.

> ## EXAMPLE
>
> In a child sexual abuse case where the offender is the father of the victim, a judge who awards probation to the offender may also order the offender to pay for the counseling or other expenses of the victim, or to pay for support of the victim during the length of probation.

Courts often require the defendant to obtain some kind of counseling in domestic violence cases. Many courts order the defendant to have no contact with the victim during the period of probation. Some may require the defendant to obtain drug or alcohol treatment, and to refrain from taking alcohol or illegal drugs.

Intensive probation supervision. California and several other states have experimented with a program of probation commonly called *intensive probation supervision*. This type of program is usually designed for offenders who need closer monitoring than the average probationer. It usually involves electronic home confinement that permits an offender to leave home only for specified reasons such as to attend school or counseling.

Supervision

For minor offenses, where the defendant pleads guilty or stipulates to the facts, the court may order supervision for a period of time, usually a few months, and defer further proceedings in the case. If the defendant serves the period of supervision without committing another offense, the proceedings will be dismissed and no conviction will be entered. You may also hear this referred to as *withheld adjudication*.

Restitution

Restitution is ordering the defendant to pay the victim for his or her economic losses. The consideration of ordering restitution is a requirement in some states, and is available whether the defendant is incarcerated or on probation.

Even where restitution is not mandatory, the judge can consider restitution for the victim's losses. The victim's request for restitution should be made in the victim impact statement. In a few states, restitution is enforceable as a civil lien or judgment. Although restitution typically does not cover the complete range of claims a crime victim may have as a result of the victimization, by enforcing a civil lien or judgment the victim can proceed with collection immediately after the criminal case, rather than having to begin the process again through the civil courts. Thus, this might be pursued to avoid having to file a civil suit.

Fines

All courts can order the defendant to pay a fine as a condition of probation, and many fines are mandatory. Court costs are also chargeable to the offender.

The Sentencing Hearing

Unless it is a minor case, or the sentence has been the subject of a plea bargain, the sentencing decision will be made after a sentencing hearing at which witnesses can present evidence.

After the verdict has been entered, the judge will usually continue the case for a few weeks for a presentence investigation to be completed, and for the state and defendant to prepare evidence as to what they believe the appropriate sentence should be. To determine what sentence to impose, the judge weighs several factors, including the severity of the crime and the defendant's criminal history. The court also weighs the harm suffered by the victim.

Special rules for sentencing hearings allow the judge to consider more information as evidence than would have been permitted in the trial, such as testimony or letters from any person who has information about the defendant's character, previous history or record of crimes, or any other information that is relevant to the issue of sentencing.

EXAMPLE

Past victims of a serial rapist can testify at the sentencing hearing to show the defendant's dangerous nature and past criminal history, whereas they would not be allowed to testify at the trial.

The Presentence Report

A *presentence report*, usually prepared by a probation or parole agency, helps the court to consider several factors prior to imposing its sentence. For example, if the crime permits a sentence of probation, the presentence investigation would iden-tify whether the defendant is an appropriate candidate, or whether special condi-tions should be imposed. Among other information, a presentence report can include victim impact information.

The Victim Impact Statement

Victims in all states have the right to provide information to the court, for consid-eration in sentencing, on how the crime has affected them. A formal victim impact statement may be the only time that the victim is able to speak to the judge about what has happened to him or her as a result of the crime. Where the victim has died as a result of the crime, or is a minor or incapacitated, it may be the only time that the court hears what impact the crime has had upon the victim's survivors.

In some states, this information can be provided to the judge directly; in others, it must be written in a victim impact statement and made part of the presentence investigation provided to the court prior to sentencing. The victim may also be able to present the information orally at the sentencing hearing.

Preparing the Victim Impact Statement

Some states require the victim to prepare the victim impact statement in conjunction with the prosecutor. If the victim is a young child, the parents of the child may be able to prepare the statement.

In a victim impact statement, you should make sure to explain to the court how the crime has impacted you as well as the other members of your family or household. The statement should cover your emotions as well as any physical suffering you have endured as a result of the crime. The statement should also include an explanation of the financial losses you have incurred as a result of the crime. In some states, your opinion as to the defendant's sentence is permitted; in others, it is not.

If no form is available, ask your victim assistance advocate or prosecutor for a sample to guide you. Keep your statement to a reasonable length so that you can present the most important points to the judge. For a sample victim impact statement form, see form 4 in Appendix E (p.162).

Presenting a Victim Impact Statement in Court

In addition to preparing a victim impact statement, many states allow the victim or victim's representative to present the statement in court at the sentencing hearing. In such cases, the statement is treated like other evidence, and the defendant is entitled to cross-examine the victim at the hearing.

What to Expect

The sentencing hearing will be like a mini-trial, except that it should be concluded in a much shorter time period. The rules are relaxed to permit a greater range of evidence to be admitted. In most cases, a single appearance in court will be sufficient to complete the process, but sometimes the hearing will have to be continued if all the information that the judge must consider prior to making the decision has not been gathered.

As you have likely discovered through your journey in the criminal justice system, you are not alone in experiencing the many intense emotions of a victim. Once your case is over, however, you have become a survivor and you can become a resource to others who are just beginning to face this bewildering process.

Contact your local, state, or federal politicians to register your opinion on current legislation or proposals. Contact the media to keep them informed on issues that continue beyond your case.

EXAMPLE

If you were not afforded your rights under the crime victims' rights laws, contact a local newspaper about improving the process for others. If your offender is about to be released back into the community, you can write a letter to your local newspaper or state representative.

Investigate your community and join an organization to speak out for other victims. Become a support person for another victim. Volunteer court-appointed special advocates may be needed by your juvenile or criminal court system to speak for child victims. Some victims have even become activists and have founded organizations dedicated to improving victims' rights. Much remains to be done before victims can truly feel that the system is more just than criminal. Find your strength, and your voice, and use them.

Violations of Sentencing Orders

An offender who violates his or her sentence of probation, conditional discharge, or parole can be subject to a possible loss of freedom. For example, if the offender was ordered to stay away from the victim as a condition of probation, but follows the victim, the offender is in violation of his or her release conditions. Notify the police immediately, and request the prosecutor to charge the offender with the violation.

Once the violation is reported, the prosecutor can schedule a revocation hearing. If he or she has not been arrested for the violation, the offender is served with a summons or subpoena to appear in court. At the hearing, the state must show that the defendant violated a condition of his or her probation in order for the judge to revoke or modify the probation. Failure to pay a restitution order or fine is not usually grounds for revocation of probation, unless the offender willfully refuses to pay.

Appeal

If the defendant is found guilty, the defendant may appeal. The prosecution has a limited right to appeal. For example, if the jury acquits the defendant, the defendant's right to avoid double jeopardy—being tried twice for the same crime—means the state cannot appeal.

Victims may have a right to be informed about the filing of an appeal, or may have a right to request to be informed that an appeal has been filed, and to be informed of the status of the appeal. The attorney general's office or a state or local appeals prosecutor will defend the appeal, and the victim can request information from that office. If an appeal includes oral argument, it is a public hearing at which the victim has a right to attend. If you do not know who to contact regarding the appeal, start with the prosecutor or victim-witness assistant who will have (or can find) information for you. Make sure you get a name and contact information to follow up on the appeals process, which can take several months to a year, or even more.

The Offender During an Appeal

Although the defendant may have a right to appeal, he or she does not have the same right to be free as he or she did prior to the trial. The defendant may petition the court for release pending appeal. However, the state will fight this request. In rare cases, a trial judge (or appeals court) may permit the defendant to be free pending the appeals court decision. If so, the same bail conditions may be required, or additional ones can be added pending the outcome of the decision.

Once again, if the defendant violates the conditions of his or her release, loss of freedom may be the result.

Make sure you contact the police and your prosecutor to get a copy of the release bond that lists the conditions of bail, and contact the police if you believe the defendant has violated those conditions.

What an Appeals Court Can Do

Every state has a system of courts designed to hear appeals. No testimony is taken in the appellate process. Instead, the appeals court simply reviews what happened in the trial to determine if a serious legal error was made. If a serious legal error was made, the conviction can be overturned and the case sent back for a retrial. If a constitutional error was made or if the error cannot be remedied, the conviction may be overturned and the case dismissed. An appeals court can also uphold a conviction, but change the sentence. Appeals are very common in criminal trials, but reversals are rare.

Release or Escape of the Offender

The release or escape of a prisoner is of special concern to the victim. Although escape creates an emergency situation that cannot be predicted, the majority of release situations are determined by the early release policies of parole boards and corrections officials. The governor of each state also has the power to commute a prisoner's sentence or pardon a prisoner.

In some states, the offender is eligible for parole, but the trend is to require more offenders to serve a predetermined length of sentence prior to release. Even if the sentence is preset, day-for-day good time permits many prisoners to serve only part of the sentence imposed.

Most sex offenders are monitored by their parole or corrections department for a period of time after their release from prison. The state monitors the release of sex offenders for a longer period of years or even life. All states have centralized sex offender registries in operation. More recently, a national sex offender registry has been established. The *National Sex Offender Public Website* is accessible at **www.nsopr.gov**. Under the registry schemes, offenders are required to regularly register changes of address with authorities upon release, and the public, including victims, can be notified. Many states have also passed laws that prohibit convicted sex offenders from residing near schools and playgrounds or seeking employment in certain types of job. Some states have enacted predator laws for repeat offenders who have not been rehabilitated. These laws permit incarceration for an additional period after the sentence is completed to protect the public.

Finding Out About the Release

Many states permit the victim some information on the prisoner's status. In most cases, the victim must specifically request this information and provide the appropriate corrections officials with a current address and phone number to receive this information. Write a letter to the department of corrections or parole board requesting to be kept informed of any procedures that may affect the prisoner's status, including release or transfer for work or furlough. See form 3 in Appendix E for a sample letter (p.161). Technology has made this process easier in many states by permitting access through the automated victim notification programs discussed in Chapter 1. By registering, you can get automatic notice of the release of a prisoner.

Presenting a Victim Impact Statement

Many states permit the victim to provide a victim impact statement or appear at the parole hearing to object to the release. This right is especially important, because the parole board does not hear the same evidence and testimony as the trial judge in making its decision. Be sure to update your victim impact statement prepared at the sentencing hearing with how the crime has continued to affect your life and the lives of your family members and loved ones. The victim's impact statement and testimony may be very compelling, and public opinion has shaped the willingness of parole officials to grant early release of prisoners. If you are not sure who to contact, begin with the prosecutor's office that tried your case or contact your state attorney general's office.

VICTIM PRIVACY IN THE CRIMINAL JUSTICE SYSTEM

10

The criminal justice system is generally open to the public. The concept of a public proceeding promotes fairness and openness in decision making. News media often assign reporters to cover police beats and trial dockets. Many people will recall the tremendous press coverage of well-known defendants such as O.J. Simpson and Mike Tyson. The theory is that the public has the right to know what goes on in the courts in order to guard against government abuse that could occur if secret proceedings were permitted. In addition to the public's right to know, the press has a First Amendment right to obtain information and report on what goes on in the courts. But respecting the media's First Amendment rights can conflict with the profound impact that the crime has on a victim's sense of privacy, safety, and security. The public nature of criminal justice proceedings may intimidate some victims from seeking justice. Therefore, states have attempted to balance the privacy interests of victims with the openness of criminal proceedings.

Protecting the Victim's Privacy

During the 1980s, the growing victims' rights movements increased sensitivity to the issue of victim privacy. Some police routinely black out identifying information from police reports. Since the press has usually obtained identifying information about the victim of a crime from police records, this can protect a victim from press scrutiny before trial. Also, some members of the press are sensitive to crime victims' privacy interests and may have an internal policy that prohibits printing a victim's name and address in certain kinds of cases, like sex crimes. (But in 1980, the United States Supreme Court decided that the First Amendment requires that in all but rare cases the criminal trial has to remain open to the public and the press.) Thus, once the case is filed, court documents with victim information become available to the press.

Victim Information

Some states have responded by enacting legislation that would prohibit police, prosecutors, or other public officials from releasing victim information to the press. Thus, private identifying victim information does not become part of the public record. For example, Pennsylvania law provides that the victim's address and phone number shall not be given to persons other than the police, prosecutor, or corrections officials without the consent of the victim.

Testimony

There is also some protection for victims while testifying in open court. In some states, a victim cannot be compelled to testify as to his or her address or phone number. Ohio, for example, permits a prosecutor to seek a court order to protect the victim from being compelled to provide a home address, business address, phone numbers, or similar identifying information.

Cameras

Cameras have also invaded the courtrooms. In some states, only appellate courts permit cameras, but in others, like California, it is within the discretion of the trial judge to permit cameras in the courtroom. Some judges protect a victim's privacy by not permitting the cameras to show the victim's face while testifying.

Your Rights and the Media

The choice to speak to the media is the victim's. Sometimes reporters can become demanding, but a victim is never required to give any kind of statement to the press. On the other hand, some victims have chosen to publicize their cases in an effort to gain attention to the crime or their treatment, and media coverage can be a cathartic experience for some victims.

If you do choose to give an interview, remember that you have the right to refuse to answer any question or set limits on the areas of the interview. For example, you can choose the time and the place for the interview. You have the right to discuss with the reporter what the purpose of the interview is before the interview begins. You can also ask the reporter not to go into certain areas, show your face, or present certain pictures. You can choose to speak to a certain reporter, and just because you have spoken to one reporter does not mean that you must speak to every reporter who approaches you. You can also decide to stop speaking to reporters at any time. If you feel more comfortable, you can simply choose to release a statement in writing to the press.

For additional guidance and information, the *National Center for Victims of Crime* has developed guidelines for dealing with press interviews and for being a guest on a talk show. See Appendix A for contact information.

RECOVERING YOUR LOSSES | 11

The cost of crime to a victim is great. The victim may have been physically injured and have needed medical care as a result of the crime. Counseling or psychological care may have been sought. The victim may move or leave a job or school as a result of the crime. Some victims may need to repair broken doors, windows, or locks, or may install security systems. Others may need to replace items stolen. Survivors may need to pay for burial expenses related to the death of a victim due to a crime.

Crime Victim Compensation

All states have set up a fund to compensate victims of crime. Each state sets out eligibility requirements and may require that victims report promptly, cooperate with the police, and file a claim within a certain period of time. All victims (and their designated survivors) should seek an award of compensation from the state crime victim's compensation fund. In most states, eligible victims can be compensated for limited out-of-pocket losses resulting from the crime. If a victim later recovers damages in a civil suit, state law may require that the victim's compensation program be reimbursed from the civil damage award.

Restitution and Reparation

As part of the criminal sentence, the offender may be ordered to pay restitution, sometimes called *reparation*. Usually, *restitution* is ordered for those offenders who receive probation, but some states mandate restitution be ordered regardless of the type of sentence imposed. This remedy is limited to those offenders who have the ability to pay and usually to actual out-of-pocket losses suffered by the victim. An order of restitution does not affect the victim's right to file a civil suit, but may be deducted from the recovery awarded. An order of restitution is protected from a bankruptcy discharge.

Insurance

Insurance may cover some of the losses. For example, auto insurance will cover theft or criminal damage to a vehicle and its contents, while homeowner's insurance provides similar coverage for loss to contents in the home. Medical insurance may reimburse the victim for medical and hospital expenses for injuries resulting from the crime.

Considering Civil Court

While the focus of the criminal case is concerned with punishing the offender and deterring the offender from committing further crimes, it is not concerned with the victim's individual welfare. The focus of a civil case is to compensate the victim. The victim in a civil suit can find out about the assets of the defendant and literally take away the profits that the defendant may have made on the crime. The losses suffered by the plaintiff are the *damages* in a civil suit.

The world of civil suits is completely different from the criminal justice system. The rules and procedures may sound similar, but they operate very differently in civil court. For example, the parties in the criminal case are the state, represented by the prosecutor on behalf of the victim and all the people in that state; and the defendant, represented by his or her attorney or appointed counsel if he or she cannot afford his or her own attorney. The victim is merely a witness in criminal court, but in filing a civil suit, the victim is in control.

The parties in a civil suit are the *plaintiff* (victim), who may be represented by an attorney, and the *defendant* (the offender or a third party), who may also be represented by counsel. As a party, the victim can make all the decisions that the prosecutor could make in the criminal case. Because a civil suit is a private action, no attorneys will be appointed. If either party wants an attorney, they must hire their own counsel.

Standard of Proof

One difference between criminal and civil cases is the standard of proof required for the judge or jury to find against the defendant. In the civil case, the plaintiff must prove, usually by a preponderance of the evidence, that the defendant caused the injuries for which the plaintiff is entitled to damages. In the criminal case, the prosecutor must prove beyond a reasonable doubt that the offender committed the crime for which he or she is charged. These standards are general concepts, not precise definitions, but the criminal standard is much higher and harder to meet than the civil standard. The civil standard of a *preponderance of the evidence* has been described as requiring the jury to find that the plaintiff's version of the facts is slightly more likely than the defendant's version. It has also been described as requiring the plaintiff to prove his or her case by slightly more than a 50% certainty.

Although it is difficult to compare the two standards in terms of a percentage, it has been said that beyond a reasonable doubt requires at least a 75% certainty, because some states allow convictions based upon the agreement of nine out of twelve jurors. Jurors are often instructed by the judge that if they are to find the defendant not guilty, they should have a doubt that is based upon logic and reason. A juror can have some doubt and still convict. The standard is not beyond all doubt, or beyond a shadow of a doubt.

Compelling the Defendant's Testimony

Furthermore, the defendant does not have the right to avoid the witness stand in civil court as he or she could in criminal court. So the plaintiff can require the defendant to testify, and may be able to ask those questions that could not be asked of the defendant in criminal court.

> **NOTE:** The following chart shows some of the differences between the criminal and civil systems.

Comparison of Criminal and Civil Court Systems

	Civil	Criminal
Parties	Plaintiff (victim) v. Defendant (criminal or third party)	State v. Defendant
Goal of the Case	Compensate plaintiff; punish defendant monetarily	Rehabilitate, punish, and deter defendant
Who Benefits	Plaintiff	People or society at large
Standard of Proof	Preponderance of the evidence (more likely than not)	Beyond a reasonable doubt (highest standard required)
Evidence	Inquiry very broad; defendant generally must answer plaintiff's questions	Defendant has a constitutional right not to testify or answer questions
Verdicts	In favor of plaintiff, or in favor of defendant	Guilty; not guilty; guilty but mentally ill; mistrial
Judgment	Compensate plaintiff for losses and punish defendant monetarily	Defendant is punished through a sentence
Outcomes	Judgment for plaintiff and punish defendant monetarily	Defendant sentenced to prison, jail, or probation; pays restitution to the victim or fine to the state
Settlement	Plaintiff chooses when and for how much	Prosecutor chooses to negotiate; victim cannot prevent settlement

The Effect of the Criminal Case on the Civil Suit

The filing of a civil suit is not dependent on the status of any criminal proceeding. Therefore, the victim can sue at the same time as the criminal case is proceeding, and can also sue if no criminal charges are filed, or if the defendant is not convicted. If the criminal is convicted, evidence of the defendant's guilt can be used in the civil case. Because the burden of proof is higher in a criminal case, more than enough evidence of the criminal's guilt has already been proved in the criminal court. A plea of guilty is admissible in the civil case. In some states, a guilty plea or conviction will establish liability and the only remaining questions will be proof of damages. In others, the defendant will be permitted to explain the reasons for a guilty plea.

Even if the defendant is found not guilty in the criminal case, it will not prevent the victim from filing a civil suit. Because the burden of proof is higher in the criminal case, there may nonetheless be a preponderance of the evidence, which would meet the level of proof required for the civil case. In other words, although the evidence was not quite enough for proof beyond a reasonable doubt in the criminal case, it may be enough for the lower standard of proof on a preponderance of the evidence in the civil case. So, an acquittal cannot be used as evidence in the later civil case because it does not prove that the defendant did not commit the crime.

EXAMPLE

The families of Ron Goldman and Nicole Brown filed civil suits against O.J. Simpson, even though he was found not guilty of their murders in the criminal case. The jury verdict in the criminal case is simply that the prosecutor failed to prove Simpson's guilt beyond a reasonable doubt, not that Simpson proved himself innocent. Therefore, the Goldmans and Browns were still able to prove their civil case on a preponderance of the evidence.

THE CIVIL LAWSUIT

Advantages and Disadvantages

In a civil case, the plaintiff chooses whom to sue and for what reason. The plaintiff can decide to settle the case, as well as the amount of money that he or she is willing to accept for a settlement. But a civil suit is not quick. Even simple civil suits may take upward of a year to complete; some can take as long as four years.

Nor is a civil suit judgment an automatic award of money. The judgment is written on a piece of paper, but if the defendant is *judgment proof* (i.e., he or she is indigent, has no assets, or has hidden his or her assets well), then collecting the judgment may be impossible. In some cases, the defendant may be in jail for a long time, so the judgment may have to be held and renewed in the event the defendant inherits, wins, or earns sufficient assets to pay the damages.

In considering your options, be aware of the impact that a civil suit may have on you. Before undertaking what may take years to complete, consider why you want to file and what resolution you would like to see. If you have access to a therapist or counselor, discuss your consideration and its potential impact on your health and well-being. Realize that the civil suit will continue the litigation started in the criminal case, and that you may not be able to put the crime behind you for some time to come. Realize, too, that there will be a financial commitment on your part as well as an emotional one.

Consider carefully your willingness to go the distance in seeking civil justice. Also, weigh the possibility that you may not win or collect money damages. If upon weighing all these factors, you determine to proceed, then commit yourself to the battle and seek the justice you are entitled to in the civil court arena.

During the pendency of the civil suit, be aware of the physical and psychological effect that it has on your well-being. Numerous agencies can offer support and assistance to crime victims. Contact the National Center for Victims of Crime for more detailed information on services in your locality (see Appendix A for resource information).

NOTE: Although an in-depth discussion of civil suits is beyond the scope of this book, the following chapter will help you consider this option. For more information, either obtain a book on the topic or contact an attorney if you decide to file a civil suit.

Procedures in Civil Cases

A civil suit filed in any court follows a set of procedural laws and rules that guide the process for the parties to the suit. Federal courts follow the Federal Rules of Civil Procedure. Similarly, each state has its own code of civil procedures and court rules. The parties to a civil suit must follow the procedural rules of the jurisdiction in which the lawsuit is filed in order to proceed with the case. If the lawsuit is a simple one seeking a small amount of damages, all jurisdictions have special small claims courts in which plaintiffs may sue, in many cases without a lawyer. If the suit is more complex or seeks a larger damage award, a different set of rules will likely apply. See Appendix B for guidance in finding the civil rules of your jurisdiction. For assistance in exploring your rights to file a civil case, you may also choose to contact the *National Crime Victim Bar Association* at 703-276-0960 or **www.victimbar.org**.

Identifying and Collecting Proof

Identification of the proof necessary to successfully prove the claim depends on the facts of the case. What facts does the plaintiff need to prove? What crime was committed against you? Who was at fault for the crime? Who contributed to the circumstances that led up to the crime? What facts exist to prove that the crime was committed? What injuries have you suffered as a result of the crime (e.g., financial, emotional, and physical)? How do you find that information? Who can provide information about your case?

Assume your apartment has been burglarized. You call the police and make a report. The burglar is never apprehended, but you learn through the police investigation that several other tenants have made similar break-in reports, and in each instance, the burglar gained access through the broken lock on the back lobby door of the building. Although there have been several similar crimes committed and complaints have been made to the landlord, the landlord has failed to remedy the situation by fixing the door or changing the lock. Through the police investigation on your report, you learn that your burglar also used the broken back lobby door to gain entrance to the building.

In speaking to the police, you may identify several potential witnesses to similar crimes, and you may learn that the landlord was on notice and has failed to take action. Local ordinances or state laws may list certain obligations of the landlord to tenants. For example, perhaps the landlord was required to install deadbolt locks on the outer doors but has never done so.

Although the property you lost is never recovered, you have a list of the items taken and you have valued those items. You also find that you are unable to sleep at night for fear that the burglar may return again while you are in the apartment. The crime has caused you to experience nightmares and you seek the help of a therapist. Cooperation with the police has caused you to lose days at work and you are forced to use vacation days to cover your losses.

The proof of a civil case will be offered by the plaintiff to support the facts listed in the complaint. *Proof* may exist in the form of the testimony of a witness or a document that includes information on an element of the civil case. For example, proof of the commission of the crime may include information gathered by law enforcement personnel. When the police arrive at the scene of the crime, a *police report* is completed, listing the nature of the call, any witnesses present, and any physical evidence of a crime (such as a broken window or pry marks on the door). Often there will also be supplemental reports that investigators or other law enforcement personnel may complete upon speaking to the witnesses or collecting items of proof from the crime scene.

During the prosecution of the criminal case, there will be testimony of witnesses and the introduction of physical evidence. The transcript of the trial can be obtained from the court reporter or clerk. Proof of the judgment of conviction can be obtained through the clerk of the court in which the criminal conviction was entered. A copy that is certified by the court clerk will usually be required by the civil court.

To prove damages, the plaintiff may use medical or mental health records that document the physical and psychological injuries suffered as a result of the crime. The victim may also use employment records to show lost income, lost benefits, or even loss of a job due to the crime. These records can often be obtained through a written request, or the plaintiff may request a subpoena be issued, ordering the medical doctor, mental health professional, or employer to release information in his or her files.

Organizing the Facts

Keeping your facts organized for easy and ready reference is essential in preparing your case. Keep a diary of events from the commission of the crime, listing who you have talked to and what information you have learned, as well as your emotional, physical, and psychological reactions to the crime. If your case is prosecuted, keep a record of the events in the criminal case. Keep all the bills you incur as a result of the crime.

The Basics of a Civil Suit

A *civil suit* is a private lawsuit brought by one party against another to recover losses as a result of injury or harm caused by the defendant.

The Plaintiff

The *plaintiff* is the person who files the suit. Generally, the plaintiff will be the crime victim. Other plaintiffs can include the victim's spouse, parents, or other family members who have suffered certain losses as a result of the crime. If the victim dies during the commission of the crime or as a result of the crime, then the plaintiffs might be his or her estate and surviving family members, who will usually be able to seek recovery for the wrongful death of the victim.

The Defendant

The plaintiff may have several choices of defendants in a civil suit. Choosing the defendant (or multiple offenders) requires consideration of the goals of the lawsuit. Of course, the obvious defendant is the criminal offender. However, if the criminal is never caught or does not have any assets with which to pay damages, then filing a suit against the offender will not result in funds to compensate the victim's losses. If a third party is a possible defendant, he or she may have sufficient assets or insurance coverage to adequately compensate the plaintiff's losses.

If a third party had a special relationship with the victim, there may be additional theories based on negligence, including parental negligence, professional malpractice, failure to maintain the premises, or negligence in hiring or retaining an employee.

EXAMPLE

An employer who fails to complete a legally mandated background criminal history check on a new day care center worker with a prior criminal conviction for molesting children may be responsible to the child victim and the parents of the child who had a right to expect the employer to follow the law.

EXAMPLE

An employer who fails to use reasonable care in screening, supervising, or retaining a school bus driver who molests a child on the bus may be held liable for creating the condition that led to the child's injuries. Or an apartment complex owner may be held liable to a rape victim for failing to provide adequate parking lot lighting or security.

Timing

Careful consideration of the proper time to file is also crucial, as all jurisdictions place time limits on access to civil courts. For example, in determining the best time to file suit, the victim should consider that while the criminal case is pending, the defendant could assert his or her Fifth Amendment privilege not to testify in the civil case. Once the defendant is convicted or acquitted of the crime, he or she can no longer assert this privilege in the civil case, and therefore can be required to testify and produce evidence.

Because the conviction may be useful to the victim in a civil suit, the victim will likely be questioned during the criminal case about whether a civil suit is pending to try to show the victim's motive or bias. Also, the criminal investigation may yield important information for the civil case at no cost to the victim. For these reasons, victims may choose to wait until the completion of the criminal case before filing a civil suit.

Statutes of Limitation

Although the victim may have some choices to make about when to file the civil suit, all states provide a limitation period within which a personal injury or property loss action must be filed. The laws vary from state to state, but many statutes of limitation allow only one or two years within which to file a lawsuit for personal injuries resulting from the crime.

Suits against particular kinds of defendants, like governmental entities, may also have special time limits or notice requirements that are much shorter than the general time limits. Check with the agency directly for any notice or form required to be filed, or check with an attorney familiar with lawsuits against governmental entities. And although states vary, child victims generally have until they reach the age of majority to file a lawsuit. A number of states have also extended the statute of limitations for adults who were sexually abused as children.

Burden of Proof

The plaintiff has the burden to prove all the elements of the lawsuit, but because this is a civil case, the burden of proof is not as strict as the beyond a reasonable doubt burden in the criminal case. In a civil case, the burden is said to be a *preponderance of the evidence*, which means there is enough evidence to make it more likely than not that the defendant did the things he or she is said to have done.

Each civil lawsuit has a number of required elements that must be proven in order to be successful. The crime victim who files a civil lawsuit is treated no differently than any other plaintiff who comes before a civil court. Knowledge of these basic elements is essential to understanding the documents that must be prepared and filed prior to presenting the case to the court.

Causation

The injury must have been caused by the action or inaction of the defendant. In the case of the criminal as the defendant, there is usually no problem in demonstrating that but for the acts of the criminal, the victim would not have suffered injury. A judgment of conviction on the criminal charges proving the defendant guilty of the crime (or crimes) can be sufficient to establish the causation element in the civil case. A guilty plea in the criminal case may also be admissible as evidence of guilt in the civil case.

Where to File

The choice of where to file the lawsuit will depend on the nature of the case and the convenience of the plaintiff. The great majority of civil suits are filed in state courts. Often, state rules permit the plaintiff to file for injuries in the court where the crime occurred, or where the plaintiff or defendant resides. The decision as to proper jurisdiction may be a clear one, but it may also be a very important cross-road in the case. You would be wise to consult with an attorney who has experience in the type of suit to be filed.

Damages

The concept of damages is very broad in civil law. In tort law, each individual is presumed to intend all the natural and probable consequences of his or her deliberate acts, but the specific result need not be foreseeable.

EXAMPLE

If the victim has a heart attack during a robbery, the defendant could be held liable even though he or she could not foresee the death or additional injury to the victim.

An award of damages may be *compensatory*, *punitive*, or both. The amount of money to award is a question of fact for the jury or judge. The plaintiff can request a certain amount, but the jury or judge may award a greater or lesser amount.

Compensatory damages. *Compensatory damages* compensate the victim for tangible losses. Compensatory damages provide recovery for physical injury and resulting medical expenses, earning capacity, and pain and suffering. The proof of damages is simple in the case of medical expenses or bills to repair or replace property, where the victim can show an exact dollar amount of loss. Determining how to put a dollar amount on past and future pain and suffering is more challenging.

Nonetheless, these intangibles can be itemized, and juries and judges make awards every day that include pain and suffering for victims.

Punitive damages. *Punitive damages* may also be awarded to punish the offender or to deter others from engaging in the conduct that led to the offense. Punitive damages are usually awarded only for outrageous or egregious conduct. For intentional conduct, punitive damages may be appropriate. A particular statute may permit punitive damage awards in certain cases. In negligence cases, where the conduct is willful and wanton so as to offend the sensibilities of the public, punitive damages may be awarded. The jury may make a specific award separate from the compensatory damage award.

Enforcing the Judgment

Once you get a judgment in a civil case, collection efforts can begin. Some criminals are *indigent* (i.e., they do not have any real assets from which to draw funds to pay the judgment amount). Other criminals are employed and do have some income. They may own a business or have other property assets that can be used to satisfy a judgment. Also, if the defendant inherits money or wins the lottery, those funds can be used to pay the victim's judgment. Finally, some criminals sue the government or the prison system for civil rights violations and recover monies. These can be used to satisfy a judgment in the victim's civil case.

Son of Sam. *Son of Sam laws* may also provide funds for the collection of a victim's judgment. These laws were passed after serial killer David Berkowitz sold the story of his murders for money. Although the laws differ in each state, they generally require the victim to file a claim based on a civil judgment obtained within a certain period of time. When the criminal is convicted and receives profits, that money is then turned over to the state for distribution to the victim. Check with your state attorney general's office to determine the status of the law and your eligibility to access any such funds in your state.

No assets. If the defendant does have assets with which to satisfy the judgment but refuses to pay, the plaintiff can return to court to seek enforcement by attaching specific assets. For example, if the defendant is employed, a wage garnishment proceeding can be instituted in which a percentage of the defendant's income is withheld by the defendant's employer and paid directly to the plaintiff. If the defendant has real estate, the court can order confiscation through a sale and levy procedure whereby the property is sold at public auction or transferred to the plaintiff to satisfy the judgment.

Bankruptcy. A defendant may seek to avoid collection of a judgment by declaring bankruptcy. There are many exceptions to permitting discharge of civil judgments. The victim who obtains a judgment will be notified by the bankruptcy court if the defendant tries to obtain a discharge. File an objection with the bankruptcy court to establish that the conduct is not dischargeable. A defendant may be able to gain some relief from the judgment by filing a type of bankruptcy in which he or she agrees to pay a percentage of the judgment under a plan approved by a bankruptcy court. In this case, be sure to participate in the creditor's hearing on approval of the defendant's proposed plan of payment to ensure your rights.

Defendant's Suit Against the Victim

While the criminal case is pending, the criminal may file suit against the victim in an effort to intimidate the victim into dropping criminal charges. Although the defendant may have the right to file a case, all states have laws that protect victims from intimidation by the defendant. Make sure that you notify the prosecutor immediately of any attempt to intimidate you. The criminal can face new charges based on intimidation of a witness. If the case has been completed, the offender may still harass the victim by filing suit after he or she is convicted and sent to prison. Courts understand the attempts to intimidate and harass victims, and while some cases are successful, most have been dismissed upon request of the victim.

THE ROLE OF LAWYERS | 13

As discussed in Chapter 1, lawyers representing victims in criminal cases is a new concept, and there are only a handful of clinics established to help victims in criminal court. However, even if one of the formal clinics is not available, there may be attorneys who are willing to work on a pro bono basis in your region. Contact the *National Crime Victims Bar Association* for a referral or the *National Center for Victims of Crime* for assistance at the resource numbers provided in Appendix A at the end of this book.

The role of lawyers in civil suits is completely different than in the criminal justice system. Unlike in a criminal case, there is no lawyer involvement in a civil case unless a party hires one. If you want a lawyer, you will have to hire one or find one who will take the case without charge. Remember that in a civil case, the defendant does not have a right to have a lawyer appointed.

If you choose to hire a lawyer, recognize that the law is a business as well as a profession. Your decision to hire an attorney may be based on the complexity of your case. Attorneys also make decisions on whether to accept a case based on a number of factors that include not only the costs, time, and effort, but also the potential for collection of their fees.

Confidentiality

To encourage people to speak freely to their lawyers, the law provides confidentiality protection for clients. This is called the *attorney-client privilege*. The privilege prevents a lawyer from disclosing his or her client's information under most circumstances, so if you have a lawyer, be honest in disclosing all the facts, even those facts about the crime or yourself that are embarrassing or humiliating. Your lawyer needs this information to properly evaluate your case.

Finding a Lawyer

The search for a lawyer can take some time and a large amount of perseverance. Just as there are specialties in other professions, many lawyers limit their practice to certain types of cases, such as family law, estate planning, or corporate law. The lawyer you choose to represent you should have some experience in similar civil cases, and it would be ideal if he or she had filed a civil suit on behalf of a crime victim prior to your case.

Recommendations from Friends

Many times a lawyer is chosen through the help of recommendations by family or friends. These recommendations can be helpful because the experience of your family member or friend may provide reliable information on the quality of service provided by the lawyer.

Referral Services

If you do not personally know a lawyer and do not have a recommendation from a trusted friend or family member, there are other sources to find one to represent you. In most cities there is a local *bar association*, which is an organization to which many local attorneys belong. The bar association can help make lawyer referrals, either formally or informally. Sometimes a recent judgment or settlement of a personal injury lawsuit is publicized and the plaintiff's lawyer's name is listed. Many lawyers now have websites on the Internet. Recently, some lawyers have started to advertise on television or radio. Your victim-witness coordinator or victim advocate from your criminal case may also be able to provide you with resources. You may also contact the *National Crime Victims Bar Association* at the number listed in Appendix A for lawyer referrals.

Law School Programs

One often overlooked resource is a clinic program in a law school. Some law schools maintain programs that take cases of public interest in particular areas. Be sure to check with the law schools in your state to see whether such programs exist and whether your case would qualify. If the clinic accepts your case, you may not be required to pay or your fee will be substantially reduced.

Attorney Registration

Every state maintains a registration of lawyers who practice law within that state. To find the phone number and address of any lawyer within your state, contact the bar association or other attorney registration office in your state. Look in the phone book, ask your prosecutor (who will also be registered), or contact your state attorney general's office for assistance. To find your local bar association, simply look in the Yellow Pages for the listing under "lawyer referrals."

Initial Contact

The selection of a lawyer usually begins with a phone call. In this first contact with the lawyer, be sure to obtain some preliminary information.

- Does this lawyer have experience in your type of case?

- Will you be charged for the first visit?

- How long will you meet for the first visit?

- How much does this lawyer usually charge for services?

Compare the answers given by the lawyers to whom you have spoken, and then decide which one to meet with for an initial consultation.

First Interview

The initial interview with a lawyer is very important. Remember that you have not agreed to anything other than the terms of the initial visit. Do not be intimidated by the thought of meeting with the lawyer. You are under no obligation to sign or agree to anything at this time, and you can take any written documents home to think about before you sign them. Also, be sure to write down any information you obtain from the lawyer. It will help you remember who said what later.

Follow your instincts and trust your evaluation of the lawyer when you meet. Do you like this lawyer? Do you feel that he or she is listening to you and your story? Does he or she appear to understand your situation? Are you treated with respect during the visit by the office staff? Your gut will tell you a lot about whether you wish to proceed further with this lawyer.

In telling the lawyer about your case, be as clear and concise as possible. You might write out certain points to be sure you cover the important issues so that the lawyer can properly evaluate your case. Be sure to bring any relevant documents—police reports, court records from the criminal case, etc.—that will help the lawyer to understand your facts.

Discuss what the lawyer believes the projected costs will be, how you will be billed for these costs, and what payment arrangements can be made.

EXAMPLE

If deposition transcripts and expert witnesses are to be retained, are those costs passed on to you, or will those persons wait until the end of the case to be paid?

Fee Agreements

It is essential that you understand how the lawyer charges fees and costs. Most lawyers are expensive, charging more than $100 per hour. In recognition of this limitation, some attorneys who believe your case is meritorious will accept a *contingent fee arrangement* in which they agree to wait until the end of the case to obtain their fee. The usual agreement states that if there is a judgment, the attorney is entitled to a percentage of the judgment as the fee—usually 33–40%—but if there is no award of damages, no fee will be due. You—as the plaintiff—are still responsible for many other costs (e.g., filing fees, photocopying, telephone charges, postage, transcript fees, and reporter fees).

Other attorneys charge by the hour up to a certain amount, and require a substantial initial payment from the victim. These attorneys feel that the victim's investment is essential and is a fair balance for the lawyer's consideration, time, and effort. Fees remaining up to a ceiling amount—such as 33% of the recovery—will be due only if there is a judgment or settlement award.

Make sure that you secure your fee agreement in writing so that there will be no confusion as to what is due and when. The agreement should clearly state whether an initial payment is due (sometimes called a *retainer*), how it should be paid, and whether there is an hourly fee rate charged or a contingent fee arrangement. The types of costs and methods by which these costs will be paid should be identified in the agreement.

If a retainer is to be paid, be sure you and your lawyer agree what minimal services are to be provided.

EXAMPLE

For a retainer of $500 or more, the lawyer should at least prepare and file a complaint and have it served on the defendant or defendants. What you want to avoid is a situation where you pay your lawyer a retainer, he or she writes a letter and makes a few phone calls to the defendant, and then tells you the retainer is used up and more money is required to continue.

Working with Your Lawyer

Once you have made a decision to hire the lawyer, and the lawyer agrees to take the case, be sure to let your lawyer know what kind of client you are. How involved do you want to be in the case? Do you want to be informed of each step in the case? Would you like copies of each document the lawyer files or receives in your case? Realize that you may be expected to pay for copies if there are costs involved. Alternatively, you may ask your lawyer to make the file available to you on a regular basis or set up dedicated Web access to keep you current with developments in your case.

Your lawyer should be able to take you through the case step-by-step to explain the procedures and anticipated timeline in your case. Ask the lawyer how often you can expect him or her to notify you about your case. If you know the general timeline of your case, it will help you understand how often to expect contact from the lawyer. For example, once your initial documents are filed, it may be at least thirty days (or longer) before the defendant files any documents in the case. Set up a method of contact that is convenient for you and reasonable for your lawyer. Many problems can be resolved by clear communications between the plaintiff and the lawyer.

Firing Your Lawyer

You are entitled to reasonable communication with your lawyer, and you have the right to expect competent legal counsel. If you are not happy with your lawyer, you may choose to end his or her services at any time. Be aware, however, that the lawyer will be entitled to payment for services already provided. Also, if papers have been filed in court, the lawyer may have to obtain the court's permission to withdraw from the case. If the problem is communication, you might try to work it out before firing the lawyer because getting a second lawyer will cost you another retainer and more expenses, not to mention the time spent bringing the second lawyer up-to-date on the case.

If you believe your lawyer has acted unethically, you may contact your state's lawyer disciplinary agency. Each state agency regulates lawyer practices. The *American Bar Association* maintains a listing of all state disciplinary agencies in its *Center for Professional Responsibility*. You can find the list at **www.abanet.org/cpr/regulation/scpd/disciplinary.html**.

If you are not sure whether your lawyer is acting properly, talk to another lawyer to get a second opinion. The easiest way to terminate your lawyer's services is to hire another lawyer. The new lawyer will contact the old one and get your file and the necessary paperwork completed. However, if you have not yet gotten another lawyer and you want to fire your current one, make sure you do it in writing, and unless you hand deliver it, send it certified or registered mail.

In the letter, you can list the problem or simply state that "as of __ date, your services are terminated." You should seek to get a copy of your file. In some states, the lawyer has a right to be paid before he or she releases the file. If you cannot pay the bill in full, discuss it with your lawyer to see if you can work out a payment plan, or contact your state bar association to see if it can assist you.

Conclusion

Crime touches millions of Americans every year. No one responds the same way to victimization—it can be traumatic and recovery takes time. The crime is also the beginning of what can be a long, confusing, and sometimes frustrating journey into the legal system.

The first step to surviving is to take care of yourself and your own mental and physical health needs as you negotiate the legal maze. You will gain strength through an understanding of the legal system. You must learn what your rights are and where to find them. Remember that the end of the criminal or juvenile case is not the end of your right to seek justice. Every victim has a right to seek civil justice.

This book is designed to be a resource to you. It is a starting place to help you gain knowledge and thereby regain a sense of control over your future as you journey from victim to survivor.

GLOSSARY

A

accountability. The legal responsibility for a crime of a person who aids another in committing the crime. For example, the driver is just as accountable for a homicide in which he or she plans the crime with the passenger who actually shoots the victim.

acquittal. A *not guilty* decision. It is not the same as saying that the defendant is innocent. Instead, it says that the prosecutor did not prove the defendant's guilt beyond a reasonable doubt.

adjournment. A continuance that suspends the case to a later time.

age of majority. The age at which a minor is treated as an adult, usually age 18.

alibi. A defense that can be raised to show that the defendant was not present at the time he or she is charged with committing the crime. The prosecutor must prove that the defendant was present.

alimony. Money paid to an ex-spouse on a regular basis after a divorce, as ordered by the court.

allocution. The right of a defendant to speak on his or her own behalf.

alternative dispute resolution. Also called ADR, this is an alternative method of resolving a lawsuit. In ADR, the parties seek a mediator to hear their case and make a recommended settlement, which can then be presented in the court and result in a resolution of the lawsuit without a trial.

answer. In a civil suit, this is the defendant's response to the complaint. It is filed in writing in court.

appeal. The defendant has a right to appeal the judgment of conviction for a criminal offense to an appellate court. The appellate court examines the record, based on the issues raised by the defendant, to determine if serious error occurred, or if a legal error occurred. Unlike a trial, no witnesses appear in an appeal, and the decision is usually given by a panel of judges after review of the records and consideration of the state's and defendant's legal briefs and arguments.

arraignment. This is an initial court appearance in which the defendant is informed of the charges against him or her.

arrest. The seizure of a person by the police.

arrest warrant. A court order authorizing police to arrest a suspect.

assault. Conduct by the defendant that threatens or places the victim in fear of receiving bodily harm.

B

bail. Bond money paid to a court by or on behalf of a criminal defendant to secure the defendant's return for court. Bail can be paid by the defendant, another person, or even a bond service. If the defendant violates the conditions of his or her release, his or her bond can be forfeited and he or she can be ordered into police custody pending trial.

bailiff. A court official whose job it is to keep order in the courtroom and, when necessary, guard the defendant while in court.

bar association. A local, state, or national organization of attorneys. These organizations often provide referral opportunities for attorneys who are members.

battery. Conduct by a defendant that causes bodily harm to a victim.

bench trial. A trial held before a judge without a jury.

beyond a reasonable doubt. The standard of proof in a criminal case that the state must meet in order to obtain a conviction.

Bill of Rights Act. These are laws that give victims rights to obtain information and participate in their cases.

bond. Usually money or another thing of value that is deposited with the court to secure a defendant's future appearance at the court. The amount of the bond is set by a judge or magistrate. The defendant may have to pay all or a percentage of the bond amount. In some cases, bond is the defendant's signature guaranteeing that he or she will return. This type of bond may be called a *personal recognizance bond.*

boot camp/impact incarceration. A sentencing option, usually for nonviolent offenders, in which the defendant must undergo an intensive training program. Most programs last for several weeks to months and are designed to permit a defendant to avoid a jail sentence.

burden of proof. The level of certainty of proven facts by credible evidence. The burden of proof is highest in a criminal case (*beyond a reasonable doubt*) and lower in a civil case (*preponderance of the evidence*).

C

cause of action. The theory or basis upon which a lawsuit may be filed.

circumstantial evidence. Indirect evidence that something happened. For example, if an offender has the victim's ring on his or her finger, it is indirect proof that he or she got the ring from the victim.

civil suit. A private suit between parties concerning personal wrongs, like personal injury cases.

clear and convincing evidence. The standard of proof that is greater than a *preponderance of the evidence* used in civil cases, but less than *beyond a reasonable doubt* used in criminal cases. This standard is used in certain juvenile cases.

closing argument. The final attorney's (or party's) argument in a case that sums up the evidence that attorney or party brought forth in the case and disagrees with, or distinguishes, the other side's evidence.

color of law. An official who is acting in his or her capacity is considered to be acting under the color of law.

compensatory damages. Recovery of out-of-pocket or tangible losses suffered.

complaint. The document that begins a lawsuit and sets out the theory and claims of that suit.

concurrent sentence. A criminal sentence that is served at the same time as another criminal sentence for a different crime.

confession. A statement by a defendant, which may be oral or written, in which a defendant admits his or her guilt.

consecutive sentence. A criminal sentence that must be served after the defendant has finished serving another criminal sentence for a different crime.

consent defense. A defense that admits the acts, but claims that the victim agreed to the conduct.

contingent fee. An attorney's fee that is due only if there is a recovery on the claim in the lawsuit.

conviction. The judgment entered by the judge that the defendant is guilty of the crime.

court of appeals. A court that considers the case after the trial is completed to determine whether the law was applied properly.

court reporter. The person who records every word spoken in the course of proving a lawsuit.

crime mapping. The process of using computers in identifying where crime occurs in a community.

crime scene. The physical location of the crime.

crime victim compensation. A right of recovery by the crime victim of certain out-of-pocket losses caused by the crime. Usually states require the victim to report the crime and cooperate with authorities in attempting to catch the criminal. The compensation comes out of a state fund. A victim usually has to make a claim within a short period of time after the crime to receive reimbursement of expenses.

crime victim's advocate. A person hired by the government or a private agency to assist victims negotiating the criminal justice process.

criminal case. A case filed by the state against a defendant for a violation of a criminal law.

crisis intervention. A service offered to a victim within a short time after a crime to help the victim obtain needed assistance.

crisis lines. Also called hotlines, these are phone lines that operate twenty-four hours a day and provide crisis intervention to victims or survivors of crime.

cross-examination. Questions asked of a witness by the opposing party.

custody. The status of being held by law enforcement.

cybercrimes. Crimes involving computers and the Internet.

D

damages. The financial, emotional, or physical loss suffered by a person at the hands of another. Damages may be ordered to compensate loss or to punish the defendant.

defendant. A person who has been charged with committing a crime.

deliberation. The process by which a jury decides whether the facts proven in the case meet the elements required by law for a conviction.

delinquency. A crime committed by a person under the age of 17. Juvenile delinquency cases are often prosecuted in special juvenile or family courts instead of criminal courts.

demonstrative evidence. Graphics, charts, or audiovisual aids that demonstrate a point being made by a witness at a hearing or trial.

deposition. The taking of information related to the case from a witness under oath. Some states in criminal cases do not permit depositions of the victim, or provide for special limits on victim depositions.

direct evidence. Eyewitness or some other direct evidence of a fact. For example, there is direct evidence of a robbery if a witness testifies that he or she saw the defendant steal the item from the victim.

direct examination. Questions asked of a witness by the party who called the witness to the stand.

discovery. The process of providing information about a claim or defense. Discovery may be in writing (e.g., interrogatories) or provided orally (e.g., depositions).

disposition. A sentencing decision in a juvenile court.

DNA. Deoxyribonucleic acid. A genetic material that is compared with DNA collected from the victim, the crime scene, or a defendant, and analyzed to determine whether there is a match.

docket. The schedule of a court. This often refers to a court's daily caseload.

double jeopardy. The right to be free of a second prosecution for the same offense. With certain limits, one cannot be subjected to multiple prosecutions by the same jurisdiction for the same acts.

E

elements. The specific parts of a claim that must be proven. For example, in a criminal case, both a mental state and certain physical acts may be required as elements to be proven beyond a reasonable doubt at trial before a conviction can be entered.

entrapment. A defense in which the defendant claims that the state or government induced or encouraged him or her to commit a crime he or she otherwise would not have committed.

exhibits. The physical or tangible items introduced as evidence in court.

F

fabrication. A lie.

false imprisonment. The act of detaining a person without the authority to do so.

felony. A sentence for a crime that subjects the defendant to one year or more incarceration.

felony review. Prosecutors who initially screen a case during a preliminary investigation by police to determine whether it meets the legal definition of a felony offense.

foreseeability. The reasonable belief that a consequence would follow an act.

G

grand jury. A group of jurors who consider a prosecutor's evidence and determine whether probable cause exists to prosecute a person for a felony.

H

halfway house. A group of shared living facilities that provide shelter to convicts who have been released from full custody incarceration or who have avoided prison.

harmless error. An error that does not affect the outcome of the case.

hearsay. An out-of-court statement that is offered in court to prove that it was true. Such a statement is generally not permitted, but there are many exceptions.

hung jury. A jury that cannot reach a verdict in the case. This may result in a mistrial and the case may have to be retried. In rare cases, it will result in a dismissal of the case.

I

impeachment. Questions asked by the other party that are designed to attack the believability of a witness.

incriminate. To identify oneself, either directly or indirectly, as being guilty of a crime.

indeterminate sentencing. A sentencing structure that has no mandatory fixed minimum sentence.

indictment. A formal charge of a felony issued by a grand jury.

indigent. A defendant or litigant who is without the financial assets to be able to hire an attorney.

injunction. A court order to do or not do something.

in limine. A motion filed before trial to prevent evidence from being considered at trial.

intent. The mental state in which the defendant knew what he or she was doing and chose to continue to do so.

intentional infliction of emotional distress. A tort that seeks recovery for conduct intended to produce emotional pain and suffering for the plaintiff.

interrogatories. Written questions, answered under oath, that are sent by one party to another in a lawsuit.

J

judgment. The final decision by the judge that resolves a case.

judgment proof. The state of having insufficient assets to pay any part of a judgment.

jurisdiction. The power of the court to decide a case before it. This usually depends on where the crime was committed and where the parties live.

jury trial. The trial in which a jury decides the facts after hearing evidence and determines whether the party has proved its case. Jury trials take place in both criminal and civil cases.

juvenile. A person under the age of 18.

L

lesser included offense. A crime that has fewer than all the elements of a greater crime.

lineup. A procedure in which the suspect is put into a group of similar individuals to see whether the witness can identify the suspect as the offender.

M

malpractice. A practice of law that is less than acceptable or beneath the standard of reasonable attorney practices.

manslaughter. The act of killing another person while acting in a way that does not rise to the level of intentional conduct.

Miranda rights. The rights of a defendant that must be told to him or her by police before being questioned. The rights include the right to remain silent, because anything the defendant says can be used against him or her in court, and the right to have an attorney, which might be free if he or she does not have sufficient assets to hire one.

misdemeanor. A crime that usually carries a maximum jail time of one year or less (in a few jurisdictions, it is two years or less).

mistaken identity. The erroneous identification of a person as the offender for a crime.

mistrial. A ruling by the judge that ends the trial, either due to serious error or when the jury cannot reach a verdict. A mistrial may end the case or the case may be retried, depending on the reason for the mistrial.

motion. A request to the court seeking an order. Either party can file a motion before, during, or after a trial. The party that files the motion is called the *movant.*

mug book. A book maintained by police of the photographs of known or suspected criminals.

N

negligence. A failure to exercise care in the doing of, or the failure to do, an act.

no bill. A decision by a grand jury that the facts presented to it are not sufficient to indict.

no contest plea. A plea in which the defendant does not contest the state's facts. This may also be called a *nolo contendere plea*. The defendant is treated by a sentencing judge the same as if he or she was convicted through a guilty plea or after trial.

nolle prosequi. A decision by a prosecutor to dismiss the charges. It may not be the end of the case or of the charges, but sometimes the charges can be refiled.

O

objection. A protest over a question that the attorney believes is improper. It is usually made before the witness answers the question. The judge rules on the objection, either *sustaining it* (in which case the witness does not answer) or *overruling it* (in which case the witness must answer the question).

offer to settle. An offer by either party to end the case through a settled sum.

opening statement. An attorney's overview of the case, made just before the start of the testimony. The opening statement is not evidence in the case.

order. A judicial decision, usually made in writing.

P

pain and suffering. The intangible losses suffered by the victim of a crime.

parole. The release from prison of a convict before the end of a felony sentence. There are usually special conditions of release, and while on release, the person paroled is under the supervision of a parole officer.

plaintiff. The person who originally filed a lawsuit.

plea. The defendant's response to a criminal charge.

plea agreement/plea bargain. To avoid trial, the prosecutor and defendant may enter into a plea agreement in which the defendant pleads guilty or no contest. The agreement may require the defendant to plead to some or all charges, and may make a specific sentencing recommendation. Plea agreements must be approved by the judge.

predator laws. Statutes that attempt to keep a known sex offender behind bars after he or she has served the original sentence due to the risk presented to the community.

preliminary examination/preliminary hearing. A hearing in which the prosecutor demonstrates that there is probable cause to believe that a crime was committed and that the defendant committed it.

preponderance of the evidence. A standard of proof that suggests that a fact more probably than not occurred. This standard is used in civil cases. It is lesser than *clear and convincing* and *beyond a reasonable doubt*.

presentence investigation. A report prepared by a probation or parole officer after a defendant is convicted that gathers information about the defendant's prior criminal background, education, family, and social situation for presentation to the court at sentencing.

pretrial conference. A meeting before trial in which the prosecutor and defendant may discuss plea bargains. A judge may participate in a felony pretrial conference.

probable cause. The reasonable belief—based on facts and circumstances presented—that a crime has been committed.

probation. A sentencing option for most misdemeanor and some felony convictions. This sentence allows the defendant to remain in the community under certain conditions and under the supervision of a probation officer.

process server. An official, usually a sheriff or other court-appointed person, who is charged with serving the complaint on a defendant.

pro per/pro se. A person who represents him- or herself in court without an attorney.

prosecutor. An elected or appointed official who is charged with the responsibility of enforcing the criminal laws in court. Prosecutors may also be called *district attorneys, state's attorneys, county attorneys,* or *commonwealth's attorneys.*

proximate cause. The act or conduct that is directly responsible for an injury.

punitive damages. The amount of money awarded to the plaintiff that is meant to punish the defendant for outrageous conduct.

Q

quash. To declare invalid. Defendant may ask that his or her arrest be quashed where he or she argues that the police did not have probable cause to make the arrest.

R

rape. The act of forcibly engaging in sexual relations without the consent of the victim.

rape evidence collection kit. A standardized method of collecting evidence in a sexual assault case.

reasonable care. The responsibility to engage in due care for one's welfare.

reasonable doubt. A doubt based on the evidence produced at trial that questions whether a crime was committed or whether the defendant committed it.

recognizance. A signature bond by which a defendant obtains release from jail pending trial.

redirect examination. The questions asked of a witness by his or her attorney to correct any errors or misstatements made during cross-examination.

relevant. Evidence that has a definite bearing on a fact to be proved in a case.

reparation. See *restitution.*

respondeat superior. The legal concept that holds an employer liable for the acts of its employees.

restitution. Payments ordered by the judge to repay victims for out-of-pocket property loss or injury expenses as the result of the crime. This is more limited than the potential for damages in a civil case.

retainer. The sum paid to an attorney to begin proceedings.

S

sale and levy. The act of foreclosing on real property.

search and seizure. From the Fourth Amendment to the U.S. Constitution, which says that people have a right to be free of unreasonable searches and seizures of themselves and their property in a criminal case. A violation of this right may result in evidence being excluded from a case, which might result in a dismissal of the charges.

self-defense. The legal right to use force to protect oneself, another person, or property against some threat or harm attempted by another person.

sentence. The punishment ordered after a conviction in a criminal case. A sentence may require a payment of a fine, restitution, or time in jail. Unless by a plea agreement, the sentence is entered into after a hearing in which the judge or jury considers factors in aggravation or mitigation. Sentences for different crimes can be served consecutively or concurrently.

sentencing. A determination of the punishment of a defendant made by a judge after a conviction is entered in a criminal case.

sequestration. A method of protecting a juror or witness from outside influences. In rare cases, a jury may be sequestered during trial.

sex offender. A person convicted of a sex crime.

sexual assault. The act of forcibly engaging in sexual conduct with a victim. See also *rape*.

showup. A limited viewing—usually on the street—of a suspect by the victim for purposes of identification.

small claims court. A court that is limited in its jurisdiction to hearing cases in which the demanded recovery is less than a certain sum.

stare decisis. The rule that once a principle is decided it will be followed in future cases.

statute. Law passed by a legislature.

statute of limitations. The time limit within which criminal charges or civil lawsuits must be filed.

strict liability. The concept that a person (or corporation or some other entity) will be held liable regardless of the intent of the person who commits the act.

subpoena. A court order requiring a person to appear in court and give testimony as a witness or to produce documents.

summons. A notice, sent or issued by the court, that requires a person's appearance in court.

supervision. A deferment of judgment in which a defendant must meet certain conditions. Used in minor cases, if the defendant is successful, the case is dismissed without judgment.

Supreme Court. Usually the highest appeals court in a state.

suspended sentence. A part of a jail or prison term that the defendant does not have to serve. Instead, he or she is put on probation and stays in the community under certain conditions.

T

testimony. The information provided by a witness on the stand in the courtroom.

theft. The conduct of taking an item of value from another person with the intent to permanently deprive the person of his or her property.

tort. A private wrong. This is often the basis for a civil suit, such as an assault or negligence. This is the opposite of a criminal case, which is a public wrong.

transcript. The official record of the testimony given by a case.

trespass. Entering or remaining on another person's property without his or her permission.

true bill. An indictment issued by a grand jury that finds that the facts presented meet the requirements of the law for charging a crime.

V

venue. The place (e.g., city or county) where a trial is held.

verdict. The finding of the judge or jury, as in "the jury's verdict was guilty."

victim-assistance program. A program where the staff is dedicated to assisting the victim of a crime in negotiating the criminal justice process. The staff will provide notice, information, and often assist victims in court.

victim impact statement. The right of a victim to tell the court at sentencing the impact that the crime has had upon him or her and his or her family. Most states allow for a representative of the victim to provide such a statement, and some states allow family members of the victim to do so.

voir dire. The questioning process by which a jury is selected. In some jurisdictions, only the court questions the jury. In others, the attorneys may also ask questions.

W

warrant. A court order authorizing an arrest (*arrest warrant*) or a search (*search warrant*).

witness. A person who testifies in court under oath.

wrongful death. The tort designation used to sue for recovery of damages against a person who killed another. The plaintiff in a wrongful death case is usually a family member.

Victim Resources

Victim Notification, Assistance, and Advocacy

Over the past few years, numerous public and nonprofit agencies that serve crime victims have developed websites and include a great deal of useful information on the Internet.

Federal agencies and national organizations are particularly useful, since they include a considerable amount of resource information. Also, many of the websites that follow provide links to other sites that can be useful to victims. A listing of various agencies, their phone numbers, and their website addresses follows.

Victim Notification

Federal Cases. The Department of Justice operates an automated notification system for all federal cases in both English and Spanish. The Department of Justice's Victim Notification System (VNS) is a cooperative effort between the Federal Bureau of Investigation, the U.S. Postal Inspection Service, the U.S. Attorney's Offices, the Federal Bureau of Prisons, and in the near future, the Criminal Division. This free, computer-based system provides federal crime victims with information on scheduled court events, as well as the outcome of those court events. It also provides victims with information on the offender's custody status and release. In addition to the written notifications generated through VNS, victims can obtain automated status information by calling the VNS Call Center or by accessing the VNS Internet site. A *Victim Identification*

Number and pin number are required to access the VNS Call Center or VNS Internet site.

Department of Justice's Victim Notification System (VNS)
866-365-4968
www.notify.usdoj.gov

State Cases. Nearly every state operates an automated notification system for its cases that allows twenty-four-hour access to custody status of offenders and pending criminal case information. About two-thirds of these are linked to a system called VINE (*Victim Information and Notification Everyday*). Because these telephone numbers are different, VINE also operates an online system called VINELINK where persons can register for automatic notification.

VINELINK
www.vinelink.com

General Victim Assistance

National Center for Victims of Crime (NCVC)
800-FYI-CALL (800-394-2255)
www.ncvc.org

The NCVC is the nation's leading nonprofit victims' rights and victim assistance organization. It is a comprehensive source of crime victimization information and referrals to local victim assistance programs, and it offers attorney referrals for civil suits.

National Criminal Justice Reference Service (NCJRS)
800-851-3420
www.ncjrs.org

The NCJRS provides extensive sources of information on criminal and juvenile justice. It has a searchable database of federal information on victims.

National Organization for Victim Assistance (NOVA)
800-TRY-NOVA (800-879-6682)
www.trynova.org

The NOVA is the oldest victims' rights nonprofit organization. It provides national advocacy and direct services to victims. The phone number operates as a twenty-four-hour information and referral hotline.

Office for Victims of Crime (OVC)
800-627-6872
www.ojp.usdoj.gov/ovc

The OVC is the agency within the U.S. Department of Justice focused on crime victims. The OVC has extensive resources and an online resource center on victim information. It also has an online directory of victim service organizations.

Office of the Victims' Rights Ombudsmen
www.usdoj.gov/usao/eousa/vr

This office is found within the Executive Office for the United States Attorneys. It provides for review of victim rights violations involving federal cases. The office provides for a complaint that can be filed with the Department of Justice. The complaint process is not designed for the correction of specific victims' rights violations, but instead to request corrective or disciplinary action against Department of Justice employees.

Witness Justice
www.witnessjustice.org

Witness Justice is a nonprofit organization that works with all types of crime victims. It can provide direct assistance to victims.

Assistance by Type of Victim or Crime

Children

National Center for Missing and Exploited Children (NCMEC)
800-THE-LOST (800-843-5678)
800-826-7653 (TDD)
www.missingkids.com

The NCMEC operates a twenty-four-hour hotline and is a national clearinghouse and resource center on the abduction and sexual exploitation of children. The NCMEC has worked with law enforcement to recover more than 121,000 children. It also operates a twenty-four-hour child pornography cybertip line at **www.CyberTipline.com**.

ChildHelp
800-4-A-CHILD (800-422-4453)
800-2-A-CHILD (TDD)
www.childhelpusa.org/child/hotline.htm

The National Child Abuse Hotline is sponsored by ChildHelp, a nonprofit organization that provides advocacy and outreach to abused and neglected children.

Domestic Violence

National Coalition Against Domestic Violence (NCADV)
www.ncadv.org

The NCADV supports more than two thousand local and state shelters and advocacy agencies that are designed to assist battered women and victims of domestic violence. The NCADV also serves as a national information and referral center on domestic violence.

National Domestic Violence Hotline
800-799-SAFE (800-799-7233)
800-787-3224 (TDD)
www.ndvh.org

The National Domestic Violence Hotline operates twenty-four hours a day, 365 days a year. Victim advocates can provide crisis intervention, information, and referrals in all states and U.S. territories.

Office on Violence Against Women (OVW)
www.ovw.usdoj.gov

The OVW is part of the Department of Justice, and provides support for local, state, federal, and tribal agencies on domestic violence, sexual assault, and stalking crimes against women. It also provides hotline numbers, Internet links, and information for victims of domestic violence, sexual assault, and stalking.

DUI

Mothers Against Drunk Driving (MADD)
800-GET-MADD (800-438-6233)
www.madd.org

Mothers Against Drunk Driving (MADD) is a private, nonprofit organization with over four hundred chapters around the United States whose mission is to eliminate drunk driving and to provide assistance to the victims of drunk drivers.

Elder

National Center on Elder Abuse (NCEA)
800-677-1116
www.ncea.aoa.gov

The National Center on Elder Abuse (NCEA) is a program of the U.S. Administration on Aging. The center serves as a national resource center dedicated to the prevention of elder mistreatment and includes the national hotline for reporting elder abuse and a state-by-state resource directory listing of agency information, laws, and state phone numbers to report elder abuse.

Fraud and Identity Theft

National Consumers League's Fraud Center
www.fraud.org

The National Consumers League's Fraud Center takes reports of telemarketing and Internet fraud and provides methods of avoiding fraud.

Identity Theft Hotline
877-ID-THEFT (877-438-4338)
www.consumer.gov/idtheft

The Federal Trade Commission (FTC) is the federal clearinghouse for identity theft complaints. It has an extensive site on how to detect and prevent identity theft. It has a step-by-step guide on what to do if you are the victim of identity theft. It also provides a form to make a complaint to the FTC.

Homicide

National Organization of Parents of Murdered Children, Inc. (POMC)
888-818-POMC (888-818-7662)
www.pomc.com

POMC provides support for parents and other survivors of homicide. It also provides local chapter referrals.

Sexual Assault

National Sexual Violence Resource Center (NSVRC)
877-739-3895
www.nsvrc.org

This resource is operated by the Pennsylvania Coalition Against Rape and is supported by funds from the Centers for Disease Control and Prevention's

Division of Violence Prevention. It does not provide direct support for victims, but can provide information and referral to local agencies that do.

Office on Violence Against Women (OVW)
www.ovw.usdoj.gov

The OVW is part of the Department of Justice, and provides support for local, state, federal, and tribal agencies. It also provides hotline numbers, Internet links, and information for victims of domestic violence, sexual assault, and stalking.

Rape, Abuse, & Incest National Network (RAINN)
800-656-HOPE (800-656-4673)

www.rainn.org

This is the nation's largest antisexual assault organization. It operates a hotline twenty-four hours a day, 365 days a year. It also operates a website that provides crisis services and information and referral resources.

Stalking

National Stalking Resource Center (NSRC)
800-FYI-CALL (800-394-2255)

www.ncvc.org/src

NSRC is operated by the National Center for Victims of Crime. Its mission is to raise national awareness of stalking and to encourage local communities to respond to stalking. It has a comprehensive website with information on laws, cases, and information on stalking.

Lawyers for Victims

A newly developing professional resource for victims is a national effort to provide lawyers with expertise in working with crime victims.

Civil Cases

National Crime Victims Bar Association (NCVBA)
800-FYI-CALL (800-394-2255)
www.victimbar.org

The NCVBA was launched in 1999. It provides technical support and referrals to private attorney members in civil cases.

Criminal Cases

The National Crime Victim Law Institute was established in 1999 at the Lewis & Clark Law School in Oregon. Its mission is to work with state and federal clinics that are funded to provide attorney assistance to victims in criminal justice proceedings. The clinics provide these services for free.

Currently, the clinics are:

Arizona
Crime Victims Legal Assistance Project
www.voiceforvictims.org

California
University of the Pacific/McGeorge School of Law Victims of Crime Resource Center
www.1800victims.org

Idaho
University of Idaho Victims' Rights Clinic
www.law.uidaho.edu/victimsrights

Maryland
Crime Victims' Resource Center, Inc.
www.mdcrimevictims.org

New Jersey
New Jersey Crime Victims' Law Center
www.njcvlc.org

New Mexico

Victims' Rights Project

www.nm-victimsrights.org

South Carolina

Victim Assistance Network

www.scvan.org

Utah

Crime Victims Legal Clinic

www.utahvictimsclinic.org

State Websites

Every state also has information on the Internet for crime victims such as victim assistance agencies and compensation programs. These websites may be part of the state attorney general sites, or may be public safety or victim compensation program sites. Many states have more than one website that addresses victim rights, information, and programs.

Alabama

www.ago.state.al.us/victim.cfm

Alaska

www.state.ak.us/admin/vccb/victims.shtml

Arizona

http://azcjc.gov/victim/

Arkansas

www.arkansasag.gov/crime_victims.html

California

www.vcgcb.ca.gov

Colorado

http://dcj.state.co.us/ovp

Connecticut
www.jud.ct.gov/crimevictim

Delaware
http://courts.delaware.gov/vccb/

District of Columbia
http://dccourts.gov/dccourts/superior/cvcp.jsp

Florida
http://myfloridalegal.com/victims

Georgia
http://cjcc.ga.gov

Hawaii
http://hawaii.gov/cvcc

Idaho
www2.state.id.us/ag/victims

Illinois
www.ag.state.il.us/victims

Indiana
www.in.gov/indcorrection/victimservices.htm

Iowa
www.state.ia.us/government/ag/helping_victims

Kansas
www.kovakansas.org

Kentucky
http://ag.ky.gov

Louisiana
www.lcle.state.la.us/programs/cvr.asp#CVR_Reps

Maine
www.maine.gov/ag/crime/index.shtml

Maryland
www.dpscs.state.md.us/victimservs

Massachusetts
www.mass.gov

Michigan
www.michigan.gov/mdch

Minnesota
www.ojp.state.mn.us

Mississippi
www.ago.state.ms.us

Missouri
www.dps.mo.gov/MOVC/Main/main.htm

Montana
www.doj.mt.gov/victims

Nebraska
www.ncc.state.ne.us

Nevada
www.doc.nv.gov/victims/index.php

New Hampshire
http://nacvcb.org/statelinks.html

New Jersey
www.njvictims.org

New Mexico
www.cvrc.state.nm.us

New York
www.cvb.state.ny.us

North Carolina
www.ncdoj.com/victimscitizensservices/vscs_victims_rights.jsp

North Dakota
www.ag.state.oh.us/victim/assistance.asp

Ohio
www.ag.state.oh.us/victim/assistance.asp

Oklahoma
www.ok.gov/dac

Oregon
www.doj.state.or.us/crimev/index.shtml

Pennsylvania
www.pccd.state.pa.us/pccd

Rhode Island
www.treasury.state.ri.us/crimevictim

South Carolina
www.oepp.sc.gov/sova

South Dakota
www.sdvictims.com

Tennessee
www.treasury.state.tn.us/injury/index.htm

Texas
www.oag.state.tx.us/victims/cvc.shtml

Utah
www.crimevictim.state.ut.us

Vermont
www.ccvs.state.vt.us

Virginia
www.cicf.state.va.us

Washington
www.ocva.wa.gov

West Virginia
www.wvdcjs.com/justiceprograms/victimsofcrime.html

Wisconsin
www.doj.state.wi.us/cvs/Victims_and_Witnesses_Rights.asp

Wyoming
http://vssi.state.wy.us/index.asp

THE LEGAL RIGHTS OF VICTIMS

Finding victims' rights information can be challenging. The passage of the *Crime Victims' Rights Act* makes finding federal laws easier. On the state level, there are more than thirty thousand laws that apply to victims. The recently completed *VICTIMLAW database* makes finding these laws easier.

The following provides an overview of victims' rights on the federal level. After that, an overview of the rights of victims in state cases is covered.

Federal Cases

Crime Victims Rights Act (18 U.S.C. §3771)

The Crime Victims' Rights Act (CVRA) applies only to cases prosecuted by the federal government. The CVRA law became effective October 30, 2004, and adds new rights for victims in federal cases. In 2005, the United States Attorney General updated its guidelines for working with victims to incorporate the CVRA. It has special provisions for child abuse, domestic violence, stalking, and sexual assault victims, as well as victims of human trafficking and victims of identity theft. The guidelines can be found at **www.usdoj.gov/ olp/final.pdf**.

The CVRA provides that victims have the following rights.

1. The right to be reasonably protected from the accused.

2. The right to reasonable, accurate, and timely notice of any public court proceeding or any parole proceeding involving the crime, or of any release or escape of the accused.

3. The right not to be excluded from any such public court proceeding, unless the court, after receiving clear and convincing evidence, determines that testimony by the victim would be materially altered if the victim heard other testimony at that proceeding.

4. The right to be reasonably heard at any public proceeding in the district court involving release, plea, sentencing, or any parole proceeding.

5. The reasonable right to confer with the attorney for the government in the case.

6. The right to full and timely restitution as provided in law.

7. The right to proceedings free from unreasonable delay.

8. The right to be treated with fairness and respect for the victim's dignity and privacy.

A federal prosecutor must notify the crime victim that he or she can seek the advice of an attorney regarding these rights.

Although it does not allow a victim the right to file a lawsuit against the federal government for violations, the act does require the United States Attorney to establish a special office to ensure that there is a review if these rights are not provided to victims. That office is the Office of the Victims' Rights Ombudsman (see Appendix A). Courts also have a duty to make sure that crime victims are provided their legal rights, and the CVRA provides for a right of appeal for a victim.

The new federal laws are having a positive impact on crime victim rights. In an appeal under the CVRA, a United States Appeals Court ruled in July 2006 in

Kenna v. United States District Court that victims have the right to speak at sentencing hearings. The case involved a father and son who pled guilty to wire fraud and money laundering. More than sixty victims submitted victim impact statements. At the father's sentencing hearing, several victims spoke about the effects of the crimes. At the son's sentencing hearing, however, the judge refused to allow victims to speak. The Court of Appeals held that the district judge had made a mistake. More information about this case and other federal cases can be found at **www.ojp.usdoj.gov/ovc/help/cvra.html**.

State Cases

There is no uniform set of rights for victims in each state, nor is there a single definition of who a *victim* is. Some states limit their rights to violent crime victims; others include a greater range of victims. But there are more than thirty thousand laws for victims in the United States. Many states protect victims' rights in their constitutions, while the rest have statutes for victims. They generally include the following rights.

- *Information* about your rights in the criminal or juvenile justice system and what services are available to you and how to obtain those rights and services.

- *Notice* of your right to know about and attend proceedings and provide impact information.

- *Participation* in terms of giving your input as to plea negotiations or providing a victim impact statement at sentencing.

- *Privacy* in criminal or juvenile justice proceedings.

- *Reparation* for your losses.

Some states also provide victims with specific rights to protection, and may provide for work-related protection for participating in the case; others may provide for prompt return of property.

Because these rights may appear in different codes under different titles and can be hard to find, the National Center for Victims of Crime has developed a *VICTIMLAW database* to help. VICTIMLAW is a free, user-friendly, searchable database of victim laws. Searches can be done by topic, law, jurisdiction, and citation. VICTIMLAW is found at **www.victimlaw.org**.

LEGAL RESEARCH

Victim laws may appear in several codes or sections of the law. To find the victim rights laws that apply to your case, see Appendix B, or do the following four things.

1. Contact your local police department or prosecutor's office for information.

2. Check with your state attorney general's office for a victim's or crime bureau or division.

3. Contact a relevant victim advocacy agency for copies of laws.

4. Do some legal research of your own.

Doing Your Own Research

Victim rights laws differ, but all are found in the cases, statutes, or codes. Also, if you want to find the charges in your case or other laws, many states have put their case law, codes, and statutes online.

One good place to start is **www.findlaw.com**. This free website compiles the links to the official databases of federal and state laws. Public libraries often make the Internet available to their patrons. This means that not only is online research a very fast method of finding the law, it is also affordable.

If you do not have access to the Internet, doing your own research means visiting a library. It is more difficult to find victim laws in books because the laws often appear in several different sections of the codes. A large public library may carry legal or government books, but you may need to visit a law library in order to find updated copies of your state's cases, legal statutes, or codes. The actual title of the book is very important.

Contact the closest appropriate library to determine its hours and location. The reference librarians can help you find the set of books you need. Some states have passed constitutional amendments for crime victims, which may be found in the constitutional volume of the same state statutes or code. Be sure to look for the most current supplement, as laws frequently change.

Many victim rights laws are found within a chapter or section of the state's criminal code. The criminal code will include the names, definitions, and elements of the various criminal offenses in your state. If you are interested in finding your specific crime and you do not have a statute or code citation, look in the index volume under the name of your crime (e.g., *assault and battery* or *aggravated assault*), or look in the index of the criminal code chapter or volume. The index will give you the statute or code section number.

Often, the statute or code books include *case annotations*, which are summaries of various appellate case decisions that have interpreted and explained the laws.

All the appellate court decisions are printed in federal, state, and regional *case reporters*. These are sets of books that contain the full written opinions of the appellate courts. To find a case that is listed in the annotations, carefully copy down the case name and the numbers that follow exactly, or make a copy of the page with the case annotation on it. Next, find out where the case reporters are in the library. Many reporters have two or more *series* (i.e., instead of continuing to number the volumes, they started a second series that begins with volume one). Also, there may be more than one reporter in which the same case can be found. Each state publishes a reporter of its cases, and there are also regional reporters that combine cases from several states in the same geographical area (as in the following example). Ask your reference librarian for assistance. The citation often looks as follows.

State v. Gonzales, 181 Ariz. 502, 892 P.2d 838 (1995).

Once you find the proper state or regional reporter, the case is found using the following method.

181	Ariz.	502
Volume	*State Court*	*Page Number*

In this example, you would first locate the set of books marked *Arizona Reports*. Then you would locate volume 181 and turn to page 502. Here you would find the Arizona Supreme Court's opinion in *State v. Gonzales*, decided in 1995. (This same case would also be found on page 838 of volume 892 of the Pacific Reporter, Second Series.)

If the case has been appealed to a higher state or federal court, there are other sets of books (called *Shepard's Citations*) that will lead you to the later case reporter citations.

CASE MANAGEMENT GUIDE

Appendix D

Case Management

Court cases may take a long time to complete. Preparation includes organizing your materials so that you have ready access to important information that you may need as you travel through your case. You may need this information for later use in a civil case, or to check on the offender's release information. If you organize your files on your computer, be sure to keep your outline updated.

Organize material from the oldest (on the bottom or in the back) to the newest. For hard copies, use folders or colored sheets to separate topics. The following suggestions will help you keep good records.

- Select a place to keep your hard copy records. Obtain a storage box with a cover, a large file folder, and a three-ring binder from an office supply store, or clear a space on your bookcase or in a drawer.

- Take every form, brochure, and informational sheet that is offered to you or that is available for victims of crime. Even if you are not sure you will use the service listed, take it anyway.

- When you are at the police station or the hospital, ask for copies of brochures and other forms for crime victims.

- Contact your local crime victim crisis center or resource center for information. Request that they send you any available information pertaining to your type of case.

- Put every sheet that pertains to crisis or emergency victim services in one file, section, or stack. You may need these hotline numbers in the middle of the night or during a crisis.

- Ask for a copy of your police report and any other available law enforcement documents.

- Contact your local prosecutor's office or speak to victim-witness personnel for copies of charging documents and relevant laws.

- Check with your state attorney general's office for a victims' or crime bureau division, and ask them to send you copies of information on crime victim compensation and other programs for victims.

- Separate police, prosecutor, and legal information into separate stacks or files.

- Keep a log for each file. Every time you contact an agency, write down the date, the name of the person you spoke to, and a brief description of the discussion.

- Take a notepad and pen with you when you meet with criminal justice officials and attend court proceedings. Be aware, however, that if you take notes into court with you, the defense attorney may want to examine them. Check with your prosecutor before you do so.

- Keep copies of letters you write to police, prosecutors, the judge, and corrections officials.

- Use a small address book to keep the names, addresses, and phone numbers of police and prosecutors, judges, victim-assistance personnel, and probation, corrections, and parole officers. Do not hesitate to request a name, address, and telephone number. Take a business card if one is available.

Throughout your case, update your records. There is no need to keep several copies of each item; one will do. By organizing your records, you will be able to utilize information in filing insurance claims or crime victim's compensation forms, during testimony, at sentencing and parole hearings, or for filing a later *civil lien* or a *civil suit*.

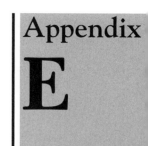

SAMPLE FORMS

This appendix includes sample forms. Use these as a guide when filling out or writing the forms that may be used in your state and municipality.

Write this letter to the officer in charge of your case. If you do not know which officer to address your request to, then send it to the police department in care of the police chief.

Write this letter to the prosecutor in charge of your case. If you do not know which prosecutor to address your request to, then send it to the office of the prosecutor (sometimes called district attorney or state's attorney or county attorney).

Check to see if you can register with your automated notification system for prompt notice of escape, release, or discharge. (see Appendix A.) Once the offender is incarcerated, write this letter to the department of corrections or prisoner review/parole board/county sheriff/juvenile detention center or mental health facility. If you do not know which department to address your request to, then contact your prosecuting attorney for information.

This statement is to be considered prior to sentencing the offender. In some states, it can be provided to a prosecutor for use in plea negotiations. Therefore it should be started as soon as possible after the charges have been filed. Check with your prosecutor for more information and to see if they have a form for you to follow or use the sample as a template.

REQUEST LETTER TO POLICE

[Your Name]

[Your Street Address]

[Your City, State, Zip Code]

[Date]

Re: [Identify your case, include police report number if you have one, or date of crime if not]

Dear [Name of individual if known; if not, address to "Investigator," "Detective," "Chief," etc.]:

I was the victim of a [type of crime] on [date]. Under the victims' rights laws of this state, I am hereby requesting that you keep me informed as to the status of the investigation. Please provide me with the name and contact number for the officer assigned to my case.

Please contact me to confirm that you have received this letter. [Give contact information here: e.g., "I can be contacted in the daytime at 555-9999 or 123 South Street, Apt. 202"]. I look forward to hearing from you.

Thank you,

[Your signature]

[Your name typed or printed]

REQUEST FOR INFORMATION FROM PROSECUTOR

[Your Name]

[Your Street Address]

[Your City, State, Zip Code]

[Date]

Re: *[Identify your case, including police report number if you have one, or date of crime if not]*

Dear *[Name of prosecutor if known, or "Prosecuting Attorney"]*:

I was the victim of a *[type of crime]* on *[date]*. I hereby request a copy of the victims' rights laws of our state. I also request that you keep me informed as to the following: *[arrest, filing of charges, bail release of defendant, advance notice of hearings, and continuances, and opportunity to confer with you before you make a plea agreement, right to restitution, victim compensation]*. Finally, please provide the name of the attorney responsible for prosecuting my case and a contact number.

I look forward to prosecuting my case. Please contact me to confirm that you have received this letter. *[Give contact information here, e.g., "I can be contacted in the daytime at 555-9999 or 123 South Street, Apt. 202"]*. I look forward to hearing from you.

Thank you,

[Your signature]

[Your name typed or printed]

REQUEST FOR PRISONER INFORMATION

[Your Name]

[Your Street Address]

[Your City, State, Zip Code]

[Date]

Re: *[Identify your case, including court docket number if you have one]*

Dear *["Warden," "Parole Board," "Review Board," etc.]*:

I was the victim of *[type of crime]*. The offender's name is *[name of prisoner]*. The date of conviction is *[date]*. Under the crime victim's rights laws of this state, I request that you keep me informed as to the status of the prisoner in advance if possible, including: escape and recapture, release for work or furlough purposes, community release or transfer to a mental health facility, and final release date. Finally, please provide the date, time, and location of any parole, pardon, or commutation procedures that may be scheduled in this case. In addition, I would like to know the name and contact number of the probation or parole officer assigned to the case.

Please contact me to confirm that you have received this letter. *[Give contact information here, e.g., "I can be contacted in the daytime at 555-9999 or 123 South Street, Apt. 202"]*. I look forward to hearing from you.

Thank you,

[Your signature]

[Your name typed or printed]

Victim Impact Statement

Case: State v. John Smith [*name of offender*]

Docket/Case Number: 2001 CR 1009

Crime: [*list crimes here*]

>   attempted armed robbery

>   aggravated vehicular carjacking

Victim Information:

Name: Rhonda Jones   Age: 46   Phone: omitted

Address: omitted

City: omitted   State: omitted

Work Address: omitted

City: omitted   State: omitted

I was the victim of: [*describe crime*]

The above crimes committed by the defendant on June 10, 2005, when defendant attempted to rob me at gunpoint, then threw me out of the car and stole my 2003 Impala, leaving me sprawled on the street.

Loss suffered:

[*complete sections that apply to your case; attach documentation where possible*]

I was physically injured: [*include description of medical care or emergency treatment, hospitalization; list all doctors and hospitals; explain doctor's treatment, therapy, etc; anticipated future physical impairment based on medical evaluation or doctor's statement*]

I was taken by ambulance to Janesville Hospital, where I was treated for a fractured hip, numerous bruises and contusions, and received 4 stitches in my head. My bills thus far total $7,500, and I continue to undergo therapy for my hip, which is anticipated to last another 9 months at an estimated cost of another $3,500. Medication has also cost $500.00 and is estimated to cost another $500.

Amount of Medical Expenses:

$8,000.00 (TO DATE of sentence) [*insert date of sentence*]

$4,000.00 (ANTICIPATED)

I was psychologically injured: [*include description of psychiatric or psychological care or treatment, hospitalization; explain doctor's treatment, counseling, therapy, etc; anticipated future counseling, therapy, psychiatric care*]

I have gone to monthly sessions for counseling due to fears I have developed as a result of the crime. Each session costs $25, and I have been to 12 sessions. I intend to continue for the next 12 months.

Amount of Counseling/Therapy Expenses:

$300.00 (TO DATE: of sentence) [*insert date of sentence*]

$300.00(ANTICIPATED)

This crime affected me personally by: [*describe emotional injury, change in lifestyle, change in attitude, change in family/social relationships, hardships endured as a result of this crime*]

Since the crime, I have not felt safe in my car. I cannot park in a parking garage and I distrust anyone who looks like they are watching me. I have had to change jobs because I cannot stay outside after dark. This has disrupted my classwork at the local college. I am also suffering in my relationships with my family members, because they do not understand my fears.

This crime affected my family by: [*describe emotional injury, change in lifestyle, change in attitude, change in family/social relationships*]

My family, especially my husband, has been severely affected by the crime. I always ask to be driven now with my injured hip. I feel as if I am not safe. It is very stressful for them.

I have incurred employment-related loss: [*include description of how this has affected your ability to earn a living, loss of job, wages, days, anticipated future loss*]

I have changed jobs due to the crime and lost my opportunities for promotion, since I do not feel safe to travel at night, which was a requirement at my former job. I have lost at least $10,000 in salary per year.

I am/am not [*circle one*] **eligible for workers' compensation. If covered, I have/have not** [*circle one*] **applied.**

Amount of Employment Expenses:

$15,000 (TO DATE: of sentence) [*insert date of sentence*]

$10,000 or more each year (ANTICIPATED)

I have incurred property-related loss: [*include description of property, damages or loss, cost to repair/replace loss*]

My car was recovered abandoned and smashed beyond repair. Its value was $15,000.00. Also, all my valuables in the car were either stolen or ruined, and I lost various music discs, files, and other valuable items that are estimated to be $1,000.00.

Property in Custody of Police: only the car and recovered items.

Amount of Property Loss:

$16,000 (TO DATE: of sentence) [*insert date of sentence*]

$16,000 (ANTICIPATED)

I have incurred other loss: [*include description of other damages or loss*]

I have had to pay for transportation expenses until insurance replaced my car.

Amount of Loss:

$840.00 (TO DATE: of sentence) [*insert date of sentence*]

$840.00 (ANTICIPATED)

Being a victim of a crime: [*include your feelings about the criminal justice process, and how you feel about your role in the case*]

Every day I experience flashbacks of the night of the crime. I feel it is a permanent part of me. I have a feeling that this will never end. The case has taken a long time to complete and this has delayed my ability to get on with my life. I am glad I had a victim advocate in the prosecutor's office to help me get through this.

Although the Judge will make the decision on the appropriate sentence, I would like to see the offender be sentenced to: [*include any or all of the following—probation, restitution, jail or prison, etc.*]

I believe this person should pay for his crime at least as long as I have to live with it. He should not be free in society for a very long time so that he can think about what he has done. I recommend at least 15 years.

To the best of my knowledge, the above information is true and correct. I understand that filing a claim for restitution does not affect my right to file a civil suit or apply for crime victim's compensation.

Rhonda Jones   May 2, 2008

Your Name   **Date**

INDEX

About the Author

Mary L. Boland is a criminal prosecutor and argues violent crime appeals in Illinois courts. Prior to becoming a prosecutor, she served as the legal director of a statewide nonprofit victims' organization. She has successfully drafted and testified on legislation, and has written and taught extensively on victims' issues. She has also worked on victims' issues as a former chair of the Victims Committee of the Criminal Justice Section, American Bar Association, and as a co-chair of the Victims Issues Committee of the Illinois Prosecutors Bar Association. Boland has served as a consultant on various peer review projects and as a practitioner expert for the various agencies within the Department of Justice, including the Office for Victims of Crime. She was a consultant on the National Crime Victims' Agenda Project and was a contributing author to *New Directions from the Field: Victims' Rights and Services for the 21st Century* (OVC 1998).

She has also written on victims' rights. She coauthored a chapter entitled "The Effective Prosecutor: Assisting Crime Victims with Special Needs" in *The Prosecutor's Deskbook* (APRI 2001), and contributed a section on victims' rights for the Criminal Justice Chapter of the *ABA Guide to Family Law* (2003). She has authored an article for the ABA's Criminal Justice magazine on cyberstalking (Spring 2005). She also directed and provided substantial edits to the ABA Victim's Committee monograph entitled *Restitution* (2004). Boland has authored several consumer law books, all published by Sourcebooks, Inc. Boland has been an adjunct professor for over ten years; she has taught at universities and for a law school in the Chicagoland area. Among the classes she teaches is a course in Victimology.